Praise for Once Upon a Continent

"Packed with eye-opening cultural reflection and gripping moments of near-disasters and engrossing discoveries, *Once Upon a Continent* is more than a travelogue and a memoir. It's a venture into wonder. Prepare to be amazed."
— Diane Donovan, Senior Reviewer, *Midwest Book Review*

"Emily Dickinson wrote, 'There is no Frigate like a Book / To take us Lands away.' Susanna Janssen's *Once Upon a Continent* will transport you to lands away with her luminous writing and passionate eye."
— Richard Lederer, author of *American History for Everyone* and *Anguished English*

"*Once Upon a Continent* brings to life a world of adventure and romance modern travelers have likely never experienced. Janssen highlights the perils and thrills of globe-trotting in the pre-internet era. She is the perfect tour guide: clever, curious, informed, and cool in the face of danger. Her charming travel memoir sings."
— Jody Gehrman, author of *The Girls Weekend* and *The Protégé*

"Susanna Janssen's latest gem chronicles the transformative odyssey of two young women across 1970s South America. Echoing the storytelling prowess in her acclaimed debut, *Wordstruck!*, Janssen weaves a captivating narrative and a vivid tapestry of South American cultures. With a deft hand, Janssen intertwines suspense, pathos, and moments of genuine hilarity, delivering a literary home run. This enthralling journey not only entertains but also enlightens, offering readers a vivid glimpse into a bygone era through the eyes of its intrepid protagonists."
— Richard Gardiner, MD, Distinguished Life Fellow, American Psychiatric Association, author and editor

"What a treat to sit down with Susanna Janssen's tales of adventure! She writes with a refreshing mix of candor, humor, and humility, and her dual language gift brings authenticity to the lively scenes. Reading this memoir sparked memories of my pre-internet travel experiences when hand-drawn maps and dog-eared guidebooks were essential."
— Carol D. Hamilton, MD, Emeritus Professor of Medicine, Duke University and author of *Hitchhiking to Madness: A Memoir*

"Susanna Janssen is the consummate adventure traveler. This charming memoir captures the places, Spanish language idiosyncrasies, and people of a time before cellphones, ATMs, and Google. Her struggles to find cash, a place to sleep, and contact with home are reminders of how exotic travel used to be. Enjoy South America with Susanna and wish that you had been there!"
— Dr. Victoria Patterson, Anthropologist and fellow traveler

"*Once Upon a Continent* is an extraordinary travel story about a curious young woman with a desire to discover a continent. She shared this desire with a friend, and the two of them set off on a big adventure. This is more than a wonderful piece of travel writing. This is a soulful experience that creates a feeling of joy. I could not put it down."
— Steve Brumme, author of *Moving Fast Sitting Still: A 900 Mile Journey to Feed the Soul*

"Susanna Janssen's delightful memoir describes her travels through South America. It recounts chance encounters and quirky adventures and invites readers to journey back in time. Wayfarers in the 1970s had to rely on their own devices rather than the digital devices that accompany the modern traveler. A compelling odyssey about a more innocent time."
— Armand Brint, author of seven poetry collections and one book on the art of writing poems

"*Once Upon a Continent* takes readers with then-29-year-old Susanna Janssen as she travels thousands of miles, visits ten different countries, and soaks up the culture, history, and personality traits of each place she visits. She also shows us how different the world was back in 1979. I can't wait to give this wonderful book to my friends who are armchair tourists or intrepid travelers."

— Marilyn Murray Willison, journalist and award-winning author of *What the Honeybees Taught Me*

"This authentic account of a young woman's travels through South America during the late seventies will delight anyone interested in Spanish or the countries where it is spoken. Janssen's colorful descriptions bring the countryside and its people to life. Readers who like to learn things while pleasure reading will find this book especially rewarding."

— Tom Jenkins, author of *The Next Run* (a memoir)

Once Upon a Continent

Once Upon a Continent

A Memoir of South American
Adventures Unplugged

Susanna Janssen

Copyright © 2025 by Susanna Janssen

All rights reserved. No parts of this publication may be reproduced, distributed or transmitted in any form or by any means, including photocopying, recording, digital scanning or other electronic or mechanical methods, without the prior written permission of the publisher, except in the case of brief quotations embodied in critical reviews and certain other noncommercial uses permitted by copyright law. For permission requests, please contact Susanna Janssen.

This book reflects the author's recollections of experiences over time. Some names have been changed, and some dialogue has been recreated.

LEXICON ALLEY
—— PRESS ——

To contact the author about speaking or ordering books in bulk, visit susannajanssen.com

Edited by David Aretha
Book design by Christy Day, Constellation Book Services
Map created by Sarah Janssen Art
Photo restoration/Image mastering: David Nelson
Author photo: Elsa Lojic

ISBN (paperback): 978-0-9983048-4-7
ISBN (ebook): 978-0-9983048-5-4

Library of Congress Control Number: 2025908760

Printed in the United States of America

To Joyce
A loyal and wise travel companion,
the even keel to my roiling seas.
I have relived this continental odyssey
with you every step of the way.
We will meet again in the ultimate adventure.

There's not a thread of fiction in these pages, but Joyce is the only person who could verify that. Everything happened just as I've told it. However, if she had written the book, it would be a different story.

"Travel makes you speechless, then it turns you into a storyteller."
—Ibn Battuta, fourteenth-century Moroccan traveler

Contents

Preface — xvii

1: Flying the Comfort Zone Coop — 1
2: A Tsunami of Total Immersion — 7
3: Living La Vida with Loco — 12
4: South with No Silver Lining — 18
5: Dos Gringas in Patagonia — 23
6: My Vision of a Volcano — 28
7: Honeymoon in Bariloche — 33
8: The Buenos Aires Blues — 37
9: Parting Shot, Falling Missile — 41
10: Potholes in Paraguay — 48
11: Reimagining Argentina: Resurrecting Gauchos — 52
12: Reimagining Argentina: Walking Among Legends — 56
13: A Fork in the Road — 61
14: Under the Southern Cross — 68
15: Bolivia: The Gathering Storm — 73
16: Luck and Love in La Paz — 78
17: Escape from Casa Blanca — 84
18: Skewered Hearts and Tourist Stew — 88
19: Tug-of-War over Tourist Soup — 93
20: Making Our Way to Machu Picchu — 97
21: Magnificent Machu Picchu — 102
22: Follow That Trench Coat — 109
23: From Pigpen to Paradise — 114
24: The Flyboys of the Nazca Plain — 119
25: Lightening the Load in Lima — 124
26: The Surfing Horses of Huanchaco — 129
27: Piropos: Sweet, Spicy, and Banned — 134
28: The Difficult Door to Ecuador — 138
29: The Galápagos: A Past Perfect Paradise, Part I — 143
30: The Galápagos: A Past Perfect Paradise, Part II — 148

31: The Legacy of Lonesome George	153
32: Swept Away	158
33: Blindsided in Bogotá	161
34: Caught with the Kilos	165
35: The Caribbean Pressure Cooker	169
36: Taking Flight	174
37: Reckoning and Redemption	179
38: Valediction for an Odyssey	183
Index	188
Acknowledgments	191

Preface

Here you are at just the beginning of our odyssey, but I am looking backward from the end of a saga finally told. I was sorry to have the story end because I reveled in reliving it, gaining momentum along the way and the confidence and conviction that I *could*, *would*, and absolutely *should* tell all.

Before we boarded the flight to Chile, if I had known in advance that I would fall into a cannibal-size soup pot in Peru, risk losing toes and fingers while traveling by train through the high Andes, and high-jump my way out of a marriage proposal in a Bolivian discotheque, I might have had a momentary second thought. But I drank yerba mate with the gauchos in Argentina, visited Machu Picchu with only six other tourists, and saw the Galápagos Islands as is never again possible. Yes, it was "the trip of a lifetime," but that cliché doesn't begin to describe the wonders, woes, wounds, and wows of my actual experience.

In 1979, I hit the pause button and exited my comfort zone with great trepidation but a heartfelt conviction that I just had to go. With my Spanish teaching career, my moonlighting waitress job, and a rocky romance on hold for months, I signed on the soft-spoken but intrepid Joyce as my traveling companion for a continental odyssey around South America before the invention of cell phones, email, internet—or rolling luggage!

I've asked myself many times why I delayed decades before writing these tales. The answer finally comes clear: Recording them just for me wasn't enough, and the unfolding of the claim that "this experience changed me forever" happens over a lifetime. All along I was waiting for you, my reader, to be a part of that experience. Thank you for sharing these stories with me. And now, with nothing else to preface about, off we go!

1

Flying the Comfort Zone Coop

In a tug-of-war, one side wins and the other gets dragged mercilessly through the mud. In this case, however, I am in the middle of the tug and could be the loser either way with one or both shoulders dislocated. The left one from the furious yanks of the indigenous woman who will settle for nothing less than the purse clamped against my side, and the right one from the unrelenting pull in the opposite direction by the intrepid Joyce who is determined to save me and my bag from the señora's violent notion of justice.

I am in pain and fear, trying to counter her war cries for retribution by stammering out the blameless series of events that landed me fanny-first and up to my armpits in her enormous cauldron of soup. When another pair of sturdy señoras join the left-side tug, the volume for vengeance drowns out my defense and Joyce's pleas.

By the time two baton-swinging policemen muscle into the crowd, I am weak-kneed, inarticulate, and praying to be handcuffed and hauled out of this tug-of-war and into the safety of a jail cell.

How did I get us into this soupy mess? Well, a few months back, I had decided to make my dream of traveling around South America come true. However, it's one thing to confidently spout, "Leap and the net will appear." It's entirely another to stand at the edge of Unknown, when everything holding you is about to disappear. Easy enough to remind yourself that "Life begins at the end of my comfort zone," but when your hand is on the knob of the exit door at the end of that comfort corridor, your heart pounds with a roaring in your ears, teeth chatter, knees wobble, and your mind spins wildly. The four corners of your being clamor a cacophony of conflicting messages: *Trip of a lifetime! Too late to turn back now! Whose idea was this anyway? WHAT WAS I THINKING?* Remembering the apex of my panic all these years later, I still remind myself to breathe.

It was late winter of 1979. We had just ended a bucolic weekend in the quaint town of Inverness on the Marin County coast of Northern California—my two best friends from graduate school, Susan and Mónica, and my boyfriend, Kevin. With the wind tousling our hair on beach walks, moonlit suppers, confidences shared among friends, and trysts in the arms of Kevin, I felt cocooned and confident. But now, the girls were heading south to San Francisco while Kevin and I were going east to the Sacramento Valley.

Susanna, Susan, and Mónica at Inverness

Both cars stop at a crossroad and we girls get out to hug goodbyes in swirling coastal fog. I will see Mónica in the Caribbean at the end of my trip and Susan upon my return to Northern California, but I cling to them both at the roadside as if that might illuminate the vast unknown of the next four months. I get back into Kevin's car.

"What's the matter?"

But I can't speak for sobbing even if I *could* articulate my fears.

It all started in a classroom at Sacramento City College where I was teaching beginning Spanish conversation. My lessons always incorporated bits of culture, music, food—anything to take the *yo hablo, tú hablas* beyond rote *ha-bla-bla* into a more engaging experience of language and life. A sweet student around my age stayed after class one evening and we chatted about travels, past and future. I'd been to Spain once, Mexico several times, and I dreamed of seeing South America. What a coincidence—Joyce did too. She was a travel *aficionada* working as an analyst for the State of California, with paid vacation time and retirement benefits, as well as a devoted boyfriend who was also a student in my class, though with zero interest in international travel.

The campus conversations between us turned into exploratory meetings, then into strategy sessions, then into route-mapping. By winter break, we were shopping for all-weather trench coats and buying one-way tickets to Santiago, Chile on Braniff Airlines, the principal carrier to South America at the time. A humorous aside: Braniff rolled out an ad campaign in Spanish to extol the comfort of new leather seats, telling potential passengers that now they could *Volar en cuero*. Yes, *cuero* does mean leather, but the ad phrase was only one letter short of "Fly stark naked" — *Volar en cueros*. The promo was soon squelched but I wonder what it did to stock prices, ticket sales, and customer satisfaction.

It was early spring in our Northern Hemisphere, and Joyce and I were readying to depart for several months in South America. I was excited and certain it would be the adventure of a lifetime. I was also scared to my core. I had finished graduate school almost six years prior and was still pedaling fast to make ends meet. I was juggling four part-time jobs with no security attached: teaching part-time at Sacramento City College and the University of California at Davis (UCD), running a summer Spanish Immersion program for the UC Extension, and waitressing at a Mexican dinner house. I needed both the college assignments and the restaurant job to cover expenses and remain independent of the parental feedbag. I had managed to save $6,000 and knew I'd need most of it for this trip. I vacated my comfort zone apartment and put everything in storage. I set aside $300 to get myself re-established and into a new apartment on our return. The rest of my savings went for airfare, traveler's checks, and $100 in cash.

A financial aside that shocks and pains: Everything seems so much more affordable "back then" compared to now, and it actually was! For example, as teaching assistants (TAs) in grad school at UCD in 1973, Susan, Mónica, and I earned no more than $370 a month for teaching one undergrad class five days a week. However, on that minimal salary, I covered my tuition and textbooks for the two years, while mom and dad pitched in $90 a month for rent and food. Today, the cost of tuition and books for the UCD academic year 2024-25 is over $60,000 (mine in 1971-1973 totaled less than $3,000), while living expenses exceed $20,000 compared to my parents' output of less than $1,000. It's a fact that in those days, rent, mortgage, car payment, tuition, and so on, took a smaller chunk from the average monthly income than they do today. A passport renewal in '79 cost $5. Forty years later, it set me back 22 times that much (34 times if expedited).

Kevin and I had been together for two years in a dedicated but difficult relationship, and I wondered how it would fare on a four-month backburner of our lives. A wise old woman in Mexico taught me the folk saying, *La distancia es como el viento: apaga el fuego pequeño, pero aviva el grande* — Distance is like the wind: it extinguishes the small fire but stokes the big one. I wondered if our flame would flourish.

A continental odyssey would be a challenging undertaking in any era, but let's remember that in 1979 there was no way to stay in touch with folks back home, let alone check ahead for accommodations. There was not yet an internet on which to Google information about the schedule of soccer games in Rio, typical cuisine of Peru, bank holidays in Chile, the weather in the Andean Mountain passes, or an impending military coup in Bolivia. From our twenty-first century perspective, travel communication in the age before internet and cell phones seems about as primitive as comparing the technology of those 1970s to the earliest years of the nation when it took Benjamin Franklin and bags of mail between six weeks and three months to cross the Atlantic from the East Coast to Europe.

On April 9, 1979, just a few days into the Southern Hemisphere's autumn, we landed in Santiago de Chile, took a taxi to the city center, and had the first of dozens of experiences tromping around several blocks while dragging suitcases (rolling luggage hadn't been invented yet either) and following leads from my *South American Handbook* to find a suitable economy accommodation. Mission accomplished, we spent a few days wandering the capital, settling into the *dis*comfort zone of our nomadic existence, and meeting and eating out with locals, Italian travelers, and an American or two.

We had our first experience with the black market when every bank on the continent was closed for the religious observance of Good Friday—the 13th! A fellow we happened to meet on the street gladly exchanged a few of our dollars for pesos at a rate we desperately agreed to without question. A lovely family we encountered in front of the cathedral toured us around the hills of Santiago in their car and then took us to their modest house for a homey evening of Chilean music and a simple meal with wine and lively conversation in Spanish.

On the Monday after Easter, to fulfill our first social commitment on the continent, we took a bus the short distance west to the Pacific Coast and the exquisite small city of Viña del Mar. There, we were soon to be incorporated into Chilean high society in the glory days of the brutal Pinochet military dictatorship via our status as honored guests in the elegant home of my dear friend Mónica's parents. It hadn't yet occurred to me that some Chileans were actively in favor and support of the dictatorship.

2

A Tsunami of Total Immersion

What Joyce and I had formulated as a travel itinerary was skeletal at best. We planned to cover the continent, and we had a pretty clear idea of the succession of countries. However, except for a few leads in my *South American Handbook* for bus routes and *residencias* (guest houses, usually economical), we had little idea how we would get from place to place or where we would stay. It was a comfort that in each of the first three countries—Chile, Argentina, and Uruguay—I had a contact among the families of my graduate school friends.

We chose Chile as our starting point because we had been invited to stay at the home of Mónica's parents in Viña del Mar for a soft landing before launching into a vast continental unknown. We also chose Chile for its geography: it extends 2,670 miles along the west coast of South America but is only 217 miles at its widest point. The waxing warmth of our Northern Hemisphere spring would be replaced by the relentless chill of autumn toward frigid winter as we navigated ever farther south in a different hemisphere. We didn't want winter to deny us the glories of Patagonia, so best start heading south *now*.

Prior to meeting Mónica's parents, I debated as to how to address them. Should I use the formal *usted* or the informal *tú*? This is an issue in many languages, but especially thorny in *español* because the practice varies among the twenty-one Spanish-speaking countries of the world. For example, many of the regions of Mexico tend toward more formality, while in Spain, the informal *tú* has become much more widely used since the dictatorship of Francisco Franco (1939-1975) was supplanted by a democratic monarchy. When in doubt, it's best to err on the side of formality, but for my meeting with Mónica's parents it seemed too stilted to call them *señor* and *señora* Moreno for two weeks. Not willing to assume immediate intimacy as in *"¡Hola, Inés y Juan!"*, I opted for the lovely custom of attaching *don* for a man and *doña* for a woman as a show of respect plus warmth when using first names. These forms of address are unique to Spanish and have no equivalent in English. The letter o is pronounced closed like the o in "don't" and not like the man's name "Don" in English.

The long-awaited moment arrives. Mónica's mother and father walk toward us in the Viña del Mar bus station. She is tall and elegantly dressed, her dark blond hair neatly coifed, and he is dashing in an impeccable dark blue suit. I can still see his snowy white hair, open smile, and sparkling eyes. I confidently greet them: *"¡Hola, doña Inés y don Juan!"* and I introduce Joyce. The señora hugs us like long-lost relatives, and then she says firmly, *"¡Yo soy Inesita y él es Juanito!"* — I am Inesita and he is Juanito. Then Mr. Moreno steps forward to embrace us as well and confirms that, yes, we are to call him Johnny and his wife Inesy. Like I said, err with formality, but be ready to pivot.

Chilean Spanish is rife with diminutives, showing up as *-ito* (masculine) and *-ita* (feminine) and not just on the end of first names, but on the end of countless common words. For breakfast, there was *pancito* and *quesito* (bread and cheese) accompanied by *cafecito, tecito,* or *aguita* (coffee, tea, or herbal infusion). In general, the Spanish diminutive can suggest smallness, as in *casita* (small house); affection, as in *mi abuelito* (my dear grandpa); or downplayed importance, as *un problemita* (a "slight" problem). In Chile however, its use is constant and is just a feature of the country's dialect.

I became *Susanita*, but Joyce's name did not lend itself to an endearment suffix. In fact, it presented a pronunciation problem to everyone we encountered. The *j* in Spanish has a sound somewhere between the English *h* and *k*, with a guttural catch at the back of the throat (San José). Spanish speakers tried to mimic our pronunciation of her name, producing something like "Yoys." Every time an official took her passport in hand he would frown and then apply the phonetic rules that work for every word in the Spanish language: "Hoi-say."

For Joyce, this was a motive for more mirth than dismay. Her true source of frustration was the language itself and her limited ability to speak and understand it. One semester in my Spanish class at Sacramento City College wasn't enough for her to understand and participate in conversations which, with the Morenos and their wide circle of family and friends, marked all the activities of our days. This was true "total immersion," and Joyce's Spanish did improve throughout our four months of travel, although her frustration never went away.

It never does, you know. It's part and parcel of taking on a foreign language, and best to embrace it as a familiar friend, albeit not a favorite one. Unless you're fortunate enough to have been immersed for years in the soup of your second tongue, some level of frustration will always be there, ever-present for the beginner reduced to baby talk and gestures to get a point across but still lurking even for the fluent speaker who wanders into unfamiliar linguistic territory. To illustrate, our host Juanito was a retired admiral in the Chilean Navy, then a consultant for the shipping industry. When we had conversations about his work or I helped him translate a business letter into English, I felt the frustration of not knowing much commercial or maritime vocabulary.

Joyce and I were getting to know one another better and finding out that becoming roommates for long-term travel ranks tops as the ultimate test of *any* relationship. Our first day at the Moreno home ended with cocktails at 8:00, dinner around 9:00, and *sobremesa* — lingering at table to talk after a meal — that continued until midnight. This suited me fine since I've always been a night owl, but Joyce had long since reached exhaustion from the late hour and the constant effort to understand words and inject a few of her own. When we finally retired to our room, I sat in the dark on the edge of my twin bed, hit by a rogue wave of trepidation. How would I manage this level of togetherness for the next four months?

The apartment I had just given up in Sacramento was my first experience of living without roommates and I loved it: the fridge and the bathroom all to myself, my choice of pets or none, decorating options all mine. Now, just a few days into our trip, the differences between us were popping up like gopher mounds in an otherwise promising garden. Not only was she the morning lark to my night owl, but I realized I'd always be the lead in conversations and quick decisions because of the language barrier, which was a more sizeable stumbling block and source of anxiety for Joyce than either of us had calculated.

In my memory's eye of that moment, I get up from the edge of the bed, reach to turn down the covers, and feel a great stirring of inner turmoil: What will the future weeks reveal for us? How will we get on? How will I meet the challenges? All these years later, I can only think, "What must Joyce have been going through?" After all, though we had planned this trip together, I had the upper hand in so many obvious ways: I could handle the language; knew a lot about the geography, history, and cultures we would encounter throughout the continent; and I had the families of my grad school friends for us to connect with. Was Joyce having her own tsunami of doubts about her choice of travel destination and companion?

3

Living La Vida with Loco

Life with *la familia* Moreno was a carousel of festive meals, parties, and outings. "Inesita" and her friends had a luncheon or afternoon tea for us at a different home every day of our two-week stay. When "Juanito" returned from his office, evenings were devoted to the cocktail hour, conversation, dining, and *sobremesa,* that lovely custom of post-dinner conversation around the table.

Carmen, the Morenos' eldest daughter who lived nearby with her husband and three children, took us for a typical day of provisioning a household, which called for visits to the butcher shop, the bakery, the marketplace for fruits and vegetables, the fish monger, another store for dry goods, and several more. This style of grocery shopping was a major reason most families of even moderate means kept a full-time *empleada*. The Morenos' "employee" slept in a small room off the kitchen six days a week and went home to her family in the countryside on Sundays. There were no more young children to care for, but Angélica cleaned, cooked, served meals, and did much of the shopping. These days, fewer households can afford a full-time maid, and the grocery shopping is done mostly in one-stop supermarkets and big box stores—ever so convenient, but essentially charmless and impersonal.

From the fish monger, Carmen bought five kilos of *loco* (about eleven pounds), half for her family of five and the other half for her parents whose household had expanded to four with the arrival of *las norteamericanas*. We had a delicious dinner of loco with curried rice on our first evening with the Morenos, and more of this shellfish in a luncheon salad the next day. In fact, we ate it in some form nearly every day of our two-week stay.

I'm reminded of the famous scene from the 1994 movie *Forrest Gump*, with Bubba extolling the versatile virtues of shrimp: "You can barbecue it, boil it, broil it, bake it, sauté it. There's, uh, shrimp-kabobs, shrimp creole, shrimp gumbo. Pan-fried, deep-fried, stir-fried. There's pineapple shrimp, lemon shrimp, coconut shrimp, pepper shrimp, shrimp soup, shrimp stew, shrimp salad, shrimp and potatoes, shrimp burger, shrimp sandwich." Though there were no loco burgers or kabobs, with loco in season off the coasts of Chile and Peru, we sampled it in a dozen or more different preparations. Since the 1980s a permit has been required to harvest loco, and its extraction is prohibited during the better part of the year.

Loco is known as "Chilean abalone" and resembles that pricey shellfish in form, texture, and flavor. While loco is only distantly related to abalone, both are large sea snails. For biology buffs, the two are of the same kingdom, phylum, and class but of different order, family, genus, and species. Like abalone, loco must be pounded for tenderness since the edible part of both is, after all, the foot muscle. On our travels farther south in Chile, Joyce and I came upon two little boys hefting a fat tire tube over their shoulders. It took the combined power of four skinny arms to swing that thing over their heads and whap it repeatedly against the sidewalk. Pulling out our cameras, we asked, *¿Qué están haciendo?* The answer, of course, was *Ablandando el loco* — tenderizing the loco.

Loco wasn't the only seafood surprise waiting to pop out of its shell in Chile. Juanito took an afternoon away from the maritime office to show us around a vast marketplace, but my only clear memory is of the fish aisles, specifically the shellfish section. As we have already seen, Chile is almost twice as long as California with an average width that is less than the distance from Los Angeles to San Diego. Fishing is a major industry, and the variety of the catch is staggering.

That afternoon in the marketplace, already well acquainted with *loco*, I met my first *piura* and it dawned on me that the world of shellfish wasn't defined by shrimp, crab, clams, mussels, and lobster alone. *Piura* (Pyura chilensis) has been aptly described as looking like a mass of bloody organs inside a rock. Had it been proffered on a plate by a dinner host, I would have sampled it out of *buena educación* (good manners) but I'm happy to have had that marine delicacy pass me by because it is said to be slightly bitter, with a soapy taste and overtones of iodine.

Juanito stopped at the stall he identified as his favorite and surveyed the offerings with a discernment that totally escaped me because they all looked alike: little balls covered with spikey black "hair," each about half the size of a fist. They were sliced in half to reveal gooey orange innards. He turned to us and asked, "*¿Saben cómo se llaman?*" I was as stumped as Joyce as to what these still-alive creatures were called in Spanish, but she knew to identify them in English as spiny sea urchins. "*¡Sí, erizos de mar!*" he confirmed. (urchin/erizo, from Latin *ericius*: hedgehog.) He made his selection, and we watched mesmerized as he threw back his head and slurped, his eyes rolling in ecstasy. Fast-forward three months to our high seas adventure in the Galápagos Islands: On a certain beach, we found the most exquisite shells I'd ever seen: delicate pink and white globes with sculpted protrusions reminiscent of Romanesco cauliflower. When our boat captain said they were sea urchin shells, Joyce and I were reminded of Juanito's ecstasy over his chosen *erizo* in the marketplace—a memory that always makes me smile.

Juanito and Joyce examining the "catch"

In Viña del Mar, family friends, Sergio and Lizzie, took us on a walking tour around the colorful port city of Valparaíso; we dined with Inesita and Juanito at the Naval Officers Club; there was a leisurely Sunday spent with their adult children and the grandkids at the country home in Olmué; we celebrated Inesita's birthday with two of her best friends, Olga and Tencha; we sipped pisco sours on numerous verandas; and we pitched in to make *canapés* for the Canasta Club where I met three relatives of the Chilean dictator, Augusto Pinochet.

Conversations with Inés and Juan were delightful, in depth, and sometimes provocative. The couple was endlessly curious about our families, our lives in California, our boyfriends, and especially about their daughter Mónica, my dear college friend who, just within the past couple of weeks, had moved to the Dominican Republic to be with her fiancé, a man of darker skin than theirs. This worried them, as they were desperate to learn more about him from a third party and uncertain that he was an acceptable choice but seeking assurance that she was safe and happy.

The Morenos were warm, authentic, and generously welcoming, and I adored them. However, there was a huge elephant in their exquisitely appointed living room, and it wasn't Mónica's love life. The military coup of September 11, 1973, ended the democratic presidency of Salvador Allende and initiated the seventeen-year military dictatorship of Augusto Pinochet. By 1979, thousands of dissidents and suspected foes of this despotic regime had been imprisoned, tortured, or forcibly "disappeared" and killed, and thousands more were yet to become victims. As horrifying as this was, and despite my inner struggle, I couldn't rail against our elite hosts for their solidarity with the Pinochet government.

The Allende years were a tumult of political and economic instability resulting in civil unrest, orchestrated and fomented by the U.S. government under President Nixon and his secretary of state, Henry Kissinger. The U.S. administration was paranoid about Chile becoming

Shopping in Viña with Inesita

"another Cuba" and meddled to the point of ensuring strikes, tear gas, and food shortages as daily realities. Inesita spoke of how she and her well-heeled friends often joined the *caceroladas* demonstrations, banging pots and pans (*cacerolas*) to protest the bare shelves in the shops and markets. When I finally found the right moment to ask her about the Pinochet regime's cruel force against Chilean citizens, she admitted it was deplorable. Then she said simply and directly, unaware of the deep irony of her words, *"Pero con Pinochet, al menos ahora vivimos tranquilos."*— But with Pinochet, at least now we live in peace. It was a peace mostly for wealthy conservatives, but did not extend to students, liberals, artists, or anyone who questioned the regime, let alone spoke or acted against it.

This chapter closes with more to be revealed about the painful irony of Inesita's words, but I leave that unsaid. For now.

4

South with No Silver Lining

Our last supper in Viña del Mar with the Morenos was an ample meal featuring empanadas filled with—you guessed it—loco, that delicious abalone-related shellfish that we had eaten in various preparations nearly every day of our stay. Inés and Juan had invited their daughter Carmen, dearest friends Olga and Pancho, and the sweet young couple I'd come to love, Sergio and Lizzie. The meal began at 9:30 and the conversation never flagged until the last guests left at 1:30 a.m. The slim volume of Pablo Neruda's early poetry that Lizzie gave me when she said goodbye is still a tattered treasure in my library.

There's nary a *chileno* who can't recite at least two lines of Neruda. This winner of the 1971 Nobel Prize for Literature was lauded for "a poetry that with the action of an elemental force brings alive a continent's destiny and dreams." Pablo Neruda belongs to the world, belongs to the continent of South America, but first and forever belongs to Chile and its people.

It's not widely known that Neruda was nominated as a candidate for the presidency of Chile in 1970, having distinguished himself as a politician and a diplomat as well as a man of letters. Rather than divide the Socialist party, he gave up the nomination and fully supported the candidacy of his friend and colleague, Salvador Allende.

The three years of Allende's presidency were turbulent. From the White House, President Nixon and secretary of state Henry Kissinger orchestrated economic war on Chile that resulted in just what they had planned—widespread shortages, demonstrations, dissatisfaction with the government, and general unrest. This is a bitter truth, and a shamefully tragic "foreign policy" strategy now long-since revealed and confirmed by U.S. historians. Eight million dollars (the equivalent of $56 million today) was spent by the U.S. in the three years between the 1970 election and the military coup in September 1973 to fund groups in opposition to Allende, create shortages of household essentials, and lay the groundwork for the military takeover.

On September 11, a group of military officers led by General Augusto Pinochet staged a violent coup to overthrow the elected government that ended Chilean democracy and civilian rule. President Allende's stronghold in the official government building known as La Moneda was repeatedly bombed by the military insurgents. Allende chose suicide over imprisonment or execution after broadcasting an address to his people: "I will not resign! I will pay for the loyalty of the people with my life."

With the government overthrown, Pablo Neruda had plans to leave the country but was ordered to a hospital for routine treatment where he died twelve days later. Some say it was of a broken heart, but on his last day, September 23, he called his wife from the hospital, alarmed because he believed Pinochet had ordered a doctor to kill him. He had been given an injection in the stomach and was suddenly feeling very ill. He told Matilde to come immediately. He died six and a half hours later. The death certificate states cancer as the official cause of death although the prostate cancer he was being treated for was not life-threatening. In the early twenty-first century, Neruda's body was exhumed, and traces of poison indicate he was most likely injected with a bacterium that causes botulism poisoning. The forensic scientists also noted that political prisoners in Chile were poisoned with the same toxin during the Pinochet regime. Pablo Neruda's house was ransacked, and his books and papers were destroyed or taken away, but the poet's voice has never been silenced.

When *los Moreno* took us to the bus terminal in Viña del Mar early the next morning, Inesita wept as her two adopted fledglings were about to take flight across the length and breadth of a continent. Juanito patted her arm, and we all said heartfelt goodbyes. It was the end of April and autumn storms were kicking up in the Southern Hemisphere. There was no chance of going all the way south to Tierra del Fuego at the tip of the continent this time of year. However, we were about to dive deeply into Patagonia, a lush region of waterfalls, lakes, and volcanoes comprising all of southern Chile and Argentina, by traveling as far south as Puerto Montt, then crossing east into Argentina. Ten hours of bumpy bus in dense, wet fog delivered us to the muddy town of Chillán. My *South American Handbook* noted nothing of interest there, yet this was an important stop, one that was written in stone on my travel itinerary.

That first evening, we entertained ourselves at the local movie theater with the subtitles of *Muerte en el Nilo* (*Death on the Nile*, 1978), based on the novel by Agatha Christie. The next day, we paid a visit to the elderly parents of my dear friend Santiago Rojas. He had been preparing for the priesthood in Chile when he changed course for America to study for his PhD in Spanish literature and to meet the love of his life, fellow student Judith who represented Spain in the "United Nations" of our small graduate program at UC Davis. I was the only one of that group who was neither a native speaker of Spanish nor had spent a year in Spain and returned flawlessly bilingual, as did my dear buddy Susan from San Francisco. We were initially drawn together in friendship because we were both known as "Susanita," were both tall and thin, and were practically the only non-native Spanish speakers in the graduate program.

In chilly Chillán, I bought flowers at a roadside stand, and we knocked on the door of a modest little house in what seemed to be a forgotten rural village of southern Chile. Per Santiago's instructions to them, the elderly Rojas couple was expecting us some time before winter set in but expressed surprise that we had actually materialized. They were more reserved than effusive, but they warmed to my stories of how their son had taken me under his wing and became the principal reason why I managed to survive graduate school and get my master's degree, finishing with a command of Spanish vastly improved over what my deplorable initial skills had predicted.

In our UC Davis graduate program, Santiago sat endless hours with me going over the papers I had written for our literature and linguistics seminars, word by word and line by line, correcting and teaching me everything eight years of high school and college Spanish had not. I was a product of the old reading and translation methodology of teaching foreign languages. To my endless shame in graduate school, I could conjugate verbs and fill in blanks, but I couldn't put a sentence together, let alone carry on a conversation. I am ever grateful to all my fellow grad students, foremost among them Susan, Mónica, Liz, Coya, Judith, and José, and our director Fabián, for their generous help and compassion, but most especially to Santiago for making me his personal project with daily encouragement and endless patience.

From Chillán, it was on to Temuco for more rain and gray skies, the perfect weather for writing Mónica about my time with her parents in Viña, and another long, loving missive about my Chilean adventures to Kevin back home. I couldn't hope for any word from him until at least ten days down the road in Buenos Aires when I could go to the post office with fingers crossed for something in general delivery. I missed him deeply and obsessed over doubts about his allegiance. I often replayed the bittersweet scene of our emotional reunion when he had sworn true love and promised faithfulness after last year's break-up over his hot tub dalliance with "she's-just-a-friend" Nicki. The prospect of three and a half more months on the road of adventure was clouded with uncertainty. Temporary separation from a lover can be an exquisitely delicious experience of longing when there is trust and truth. But in their absence, doubt gnaws.

The next morning, we took a bus for a day trip to Villarica which, according to my *South American Handbook*, was a picturesque town on the shores of a vast and beautiful lake at the base of a magnificent volcano, both of the same name as the town. We arrived in late morning and stepped off the bus into a thick, cold, dense cloud. Hard rain pelted our hooded trench coats as we scooted for shelter into the doorway of a café. I'd never seen a volcano in my life, and Villarica was refusing to reveal itself. I was dejected and life felt unfair. ("Acceptance" and "surrender" were not yet part of my emotional vocabulary.) We walked a block, glanced at the misty gray expanse of lake, then repaired to the café to watch a soap opera and eat lunch.

Back in our unheated room in nearby Temuco that night, wind howled and rain lashed. Distracted from sleep, I still couldn't let go of the denied volcano experience I so coveted. But I tried: "Hrumpf! Volcanoes, how could they look like those silly drawings in a kid's picture books anyway?! Perfectly conical with a snow-capped summit? Give me a break!

Nature was right around the next continental corner with a gift I treasure and a lesson I have never forgotten.

5

Dos Gringas in Patagonia

Three hours farther south in Chile, things started looking more cheerful. The city of Valdivia glowed with sunshine, its wide river sparkled, and my optimism and sense of adventure rebounded from the dark, damp disappointment of Temuco and Villarica. I let go of that unseen volcano, and Joyce and I threw ourselves wholeheartedly into the present moment of—wait a minute here! Where *are* we? Did that bus take a wrong turn and land us in Bavaria? The map said Valdivia but the architecture of the surrounding buildings was distinctly German, the signs were in German, and I half-expected to see a tall blond lad in leiderhosen emerge yodeling from one of the chalets.

There were two restaurants before our hungry eyes: Das Haus and München. We took a table at the latter and considered the lunch special of bratwurst, potatoes, and . . . *chucrut*? Hmm, what an odd word. It wasn't in the dictionary, though the waiter insisted it was Spanish but couldn't clarify anything beyond *cabbage*. When the plates arrived, one whiff was all it took to resolve the mystery of chucrut, and my mouth was not watering. It was a smell I remembered all too well from my childhood. My Dutch father loved the stuff, so my Italian mother served it hot as a side dish. I had put twelve years and thousands of miles between me and sauerkraut, but in the Southern Cone of South America, it had found me again. There had been no escaping it at the family dinner table, and here in southern Chile it was a mealtime staple as much as loco had been back with Inesita and Juanito in Viña del Mar.

I had read in my *South American Handbook* of the German influence in this part of Chile, but there had been immigrations from all over Europe. I was unprepared for the cultural, architectural, culinary, and linguistic surprises that made it seem I had stepped off the bus into Germany. The "Father of Chile" is Bernardo O'Higgins, of Irish descent; the dictator Pinochet was of French descent; and many Scots arrived to herd sheep in these parts. Nineteenth-century Chile was also home to Italians, Portuguese, Croatians, Dutch, Belgians, Russians, Scandinavians, Greeks, Poles, Swiss, Spanish, British, *and* Americans. However, this German thing went deep and so did I to find out why.

In sparsely populated Chile of 1850, two factors coincided to pave the way for thousands of German immigrants to make it their new home. The Chilean government, worried about incursions from European regimes, was laying plans for controled colonization of the South. Thus, a law was passed to allow for the recruitment of immigrants who could claim unoccupied lands as homesteaders. The second factor was the 1848 Revolution in the German states which motivated many economically independent artisans, farmers, and merchants to leave the homeland and put down new roots in Chile. Carlos Anwandter, a German political exile and leader of the first contingent of German immigrants to Chile, formulated this oath: "We shall be honest and laborious Chileans as the best of them, we shall defend our adopted country joining in the ranks of our new countrymen, against any foreign oppression and with the decision and firmness of the man that defends his country, his family and his interests. Never will the country that adopts us as its children have reason to repent of such illustrated, human and generous proceeding."

Now, many years after my visit to Valdivia, I again ponder what an arduous and formidable experience it must be to move self and family from one's native habitat to a new country that is not only foreign in culture and language, but is a wild frontier of inconveniences and unknowns, with predatory animals, harsh conditions, and indigenous people who just may believe that this land being so freely given away is rightfully theirs. As Americans in the twenty-first century, we can hope not to experience a life upheaval of this kind, but today there are countless peoples under persecution and duress worldwide who seek a land that will welcome, accept, and nurture them with respect and opportunities.

Feeling sluggish after that heavy German meal, Joyce and I roused ourselves to tramp through town and out into the lush countryside. Back at the plaza in the late afternoon we chatted with four little girls playing around the fountain. We bought six bananas at the grocer's on the square, but when we gave four to the girls the clerk came outside with wagging finger and harsh words, accusing us of encouraging kids to beg on the streets. I commented to her that these were school girls and not beggars, and that the bananas were delicious nutrition after a long day in the classroom. Joyce and I gathered the girls and went to the other side of the plaza to enjoy the snack and have our picture taken by a mustachioed street photographer in a long white lab coat and a jaunty hat. He arranged us on the bench, bent over his big box camera balanced on a tall tripod and snapped our picture.. We must have given it to the girls for, though I save everything, I don't recall ever having it in my possession.

The next day, we had tickets for the 3:00 p.m. bus to head farther south to Puerto Montt, but there was plenty of time for an excursion so we took the morning launch across the wide sun-lit bay to the

Street photographer in Valdivia

seaport village of Corral. Chatting with the owner of the first shop we visited there, our hair stood on end when she announced that there wouldn't be another boat back until 4:00 p.m. We raced down to the dock where we had just disembarked, only to see the launch fifty yards off shore heading back to Valdivia. There was someone on deck, but I couldn't muster the chutzpah to jump up and down and scream the Spanish version of "Stop! Stop!"

Maybe it wasn't rare for unprepared tourists to be stranded on the dock in Corral, because two friendly fellows with bulging biceps were conventiently nearby to herd Joyce and me into their rowboat and ferry us out to the launch which stopped to accomodate our late arrival. We gave our rowboat ferrymen ample pesos along with

Our rowboat ferrymen

our effusive thanks and climbed aboard, relieved and laughing at our naive mistake and the good luck that set it right.

Our morning excursion aborted, we now had time to kill in Valdivia. The sun was shining but the air had an icy bite, and we were about to head farther south into the Patagonia autumn. My all-purpose, flannel-lined trench coat was a wise and practical approach to the climate challenges of seven latitudes, four longitudes, and limited baggage, but in these first three weeks of travel, I'd felt more cold than comfort. I bought a thick alpaca cardigan and a wooly cap in a local shop, then we boarded the bus in the general direction of Antarctica for Puerto Montt, our final destination in Chile.

6

My Vision of a Volcano

Joyce never complained about my smoking habit, or anything else for that matter. With three weeks of travel behind us and over three months ahead, we were settling into a level of comfort with each other on the road. Perhaps we'd never become best friends but we were bonding over mutual support and shared enjoyments. We were adapting to the other's ways and enjoying companionship in a grand adventure of different experiences in every aspect of life at practically every moment: customs, language, food, acquaintances, money, laws, transportation, schedules, bathroom plumbing, and the dearth of hot water.

In those days, I wasn't even embarrassed about being a smoker. Now I cringe when I think of how graciously Joyce put up with my cigarettes. Even though back then "everyone" smoked everywhere—in restaurants, department stores (even in dressing rooms), offices and college classrooms, on planes, buses, and all other manner of transportation, I think of how awful that must have been for non-smokers. I hadn't kicked the addiction yet and I wasn't going to try during the trip because it was a crutch that soothed the stress and eased the loneliness of being cut off from family, friends, and the boyfriend. Yes, I took great and guiltless pleasure in lighting up during our morning, afternoon, and evening coffees, but I planned to quit at the end of our trip and rush smoke-free into Kevin's arms.

Puerto Montt, our last Chilean destination before crossing east into Argentinean Patagonia, was a working seaside village—picturesque, but cold, damp, and smelling of fish. It was also the gateway to a magically transformative experience that has become my lifelong metaphor for choosing belief over disillusionment. This was not one of the wild, funny, or hair-raising episodes awaiting this fearless duo farther out on the South American road. Rather, it was more like my own private "Cinderella moment."

Just as there are more forests and rivers as one goes farther north in our hemisphere, here in the Southern Hemisphere as we traveled south, there was an ever-greater abundance of lakes, mountains, and waterfalls. And there were volcanoes—at least according to the map. This was the legendary Lake District of Chilean Patagonia, and Joyce and I signed up for a tour of the Petrohué waterfalls, Lakes Llanquihue and Todos Santos, and the promise of a volcano sighting. It would be glorious to see one that lived up to its name and fame, but the disappointment of Villarica still smarted, and cynicism was my shield against another letdown. I was circumspect, refusing to give rein to runaway hope or unbridled enthusiasm.

After two spectacular stops on the tour, I got off the bus for the third, thinking to see another waterfall or thrashing river and found myself gazing up in astonishment at the eternally snow-capped Osorno, perfectly conical against radiant blue. The sky was endless except for a single cloud clinging to the high slope of the volcano. After just that first view, whatever was left of my crumbling cynicism was washed away by the lake at my feet. It was so truly the color of emeralds that, until this writing, I'd completely forgotten that its true name is Todos Santos (All Saints) for I had always remembered it as "Lago Esmeralda" for its intense, unbelievably clear emerald color.

Joyce's magnificent photo of "my" Osorno Volcano

I walked the shores of the lake steeped in gratitude for the perfect volcano whose presence made the disillusionments of my still-young life melt away. It's hard to describe a moment like this because, in the physical universe, nothing actually *happened*, but I was brought to my emotional knees by a sight that turned out to be far better than the wildest dreams I had been trying to give up on. It was as unexpected in my world as a fire-breathing dragon, a prancing unicorn, an angel fluttering to my doorstep on silvery wings, or a Jesus statue coming to life.

When I was little, I believed I could make things happen if I wished fervently, if I tried hard enough. My childhood was steeped in religious stories of Catholic saints having supernatural experiences, and of Jesus walking on water and raising the dead. Maybe I was just gullible and naive but I thought if I truly and purely intended it, the statue of Mother Mary would come to life, Jesus on the cross would turn his face to me, and I would wake up in the morning to see the perpetual deep frown of my Emmett Kelly clown doll transformed into a happy smile. I was the kid who believed she could catch a bird by putting salt on its tail, and I chased robins around the front yard with a saltshaker for most of two summers. I jumped out of our orchard walnut tree sure that, in a moment of perfect desire, I would fly.

Later in life, as I was about to graduate from university and celebrate my 21st birthday, I believed that upon this landmark occasion, my personal struggles and confusions would simply cease to exist, magically swept away as real adulthood came swooshing in at age twenty-one. Eight years later on this South American odyssey, I was carrying plenty of baggage in addition to that one very unwieldy suitcase: uncertainties as to my professional future, financial pressures, being with a travel companion 24/7 while longing for my accustomed space and privacy, mood swings and skin irritations, the stress of living in a second language that I managed well but not perfectly, and worries about my future with Kevin. What would these months of absence do to "us"? Would he wait for me? There was a long road ahead and much to be revealed.

I realize that my volcano vision is romantic and metaphoric, incongruent with the disaster of major eruptions that threaten life and livelihood. Even so, every time I look at the photo of Osorno, I am inspired to think grandly and believe big, although no more bringing statues to life or turning rubber frowns to smiles. The image and the memory that Osorno conjure flood me with tranquility and fill me with possibility. On that day in Chile, I knew that miracles are real; that cynicism serves nothing; that all is, was, and will be well—on the trip, upon my return, and beyond. But there remains that cloud that perpetually clings to the snow cap in Joyce's magnificent photo of Osorno, and my vision can temporarily fade and become obscured by, you know, all manner of stuff.

In subsequent trips to Ecuador, I've seen a few more volcanoes, and I even hiked with one of my travel groups to the base camp of Cotopaxi's 19,347 feet. But, like a first love, Osorno lives in my heart forever.

I gaze at the photo on my desktop. I enter the image. The wind on my face, the gravel crunching under my feet. I smell pine. I see emeralds.

I touch eternal snow.

… 7

Honeymoon in Bariloche

The two weeks we were to spend in Argentina began with that breathtakingly beautiful bus ride across Chilean Patagonia followed by an unpleasant incident at the customs office entering Argentina. The dispute over the borders of Argentine vs. Chilean Patagonia had again heated up between the two countries, along with their claims to parts of Antarctica.[1]

The border official was brusque and relentless. In those days before internet, the result was worse than a mere inconvenience for me. When all the maps and articles I had gathered about Argentina and Chile had been confiscated, I felt violated and wronged, but I shut up because my high-alert radar warned me that I had something irreplaceable in my possession that we could not continue the trip without. I handed over the printed materials that were suspected of references to or images of more land for Chile and less for Argentina,

---

1 While Patagonia forms part of Chile and part of Argentina, Antarctica does not "belong" to any country or countries. However, seven countries have binding territorial claims on Antarctica, the only continent that does not have a native population. It is governed by an international partnership formed by the Antarctic Treaty of 1959, which sought to resolve decades of conflict over various nations making claims to parts of the continent since the early 1800s. The treaty banned military conflict and established international scientific collaboration, essentially dedicating Antarctica to peace and science. The treaty was signed by fifty-four nations, including the seven with territorial claims for which the continent was divvied up like a pie: Argentina, Australia, Chile, France, New Zealand, Norway, and the United Kingdom. Australia with 42 per cent commands the biggest piece of the pie.

but I held my breath until we had been waved all the way through customs. Thanks to the powers that be, I was still clutching my most indispensable possession. Had they confiscated the *South American Handbook* I would have seriously considered cutting our trip short because our day-to-day guidance was within those five hundred pages and not just a click away on a twenty-first-century device. We were waved through the border crossing, but for unknown reasons, the two Swiss girls we'd met on our bus were detained at the border and denied entry into Argentina.

Arriving in Bariloche, Joyce and I felt cheered by glittering lakes, towering mountains, and the charm of this unique village in Argentine Patagonia that looked and felt like a burg in the Bavarian Alps, reflecting the influence of the nineteenth-century German colonization in the Southern Cone of South America.

At the Viejo Munich restaurant, we lunched on the predictable chucrut (sauerkraut) to accompany the bratwurst, but our appetite for German food was waning and we later opted for a dinner of what Argentina was *really* famous for: grilled beef. Neither of us consumed a lot of red meat, and our budget was such that we couldn't afford steak dinners even if we wanted them. In this early part of our trip, we were establishing our preference for local dishes in simple eateries to sample the culinary part of each country's culture. During the Chile to Argentina crossing and during every new country approach that followed, we pored over the *Handbook* in anticipation of local specialties at recommended cafés, thankful to guardian angels and whatever karma we had racked up to still have the precious book in our hands.

At the Restaurante Europa in Bariloche, the beef dishes were so cheap that we treated ourselves to a luxurious dinner of filet mignon with potatoes and vegetables, plus the ultimate luxury of a half bottle of wine. The bill for two was $12. The prices were so amazing that

I recorded them in dollar equivalents in my journal: T-bone steak, $2.20; filet mignon, $3.90. However, with chocolate mousse at $2.50, and coffee with ice cream $3.50, we skipped dessert.

Aside from cheap and abundant steaks, I was charmed by my first impressions of Argentina. Bariloche was picturesque and small, yet already quite international, being a popular resort and legendary destination for its lakes, mountains, waterfalls, and forests. Joyce and I rode a tram to the top of the ski resort (no snow yet) and took in a stunning panorama while we munched on our authentic Argentine lunch of empanadas filled with a savory-sweet mixture of beef and raisins. We talked, dined, shopped, toured, and sampled the famous Bariloche chocolate with locals, Brazilians, Italians, Danes, and the two Swiss girls delivered to Bariloche three days after their border fiasco while leaving Chile.

When Joyce and I signed up for an excursion to the countryside, how could we have known that all eighteen of our fellow passengers were Argentine newlyweds on a honeymoon tour? Since the only others on the bus were the two of us and the bus drivers, the nine couples were soon cracking jokes and making wildly suggestive proposals that we seize serendipity, stop at the first church to have the local priest marry Joyce and me to the two bus drivers, and then honeymoon on with them into the sunset.

"But we must get to know them first to choose the one we prefer," I protested.

"No worries," they countered, "you can always switch off later!"

They accompanied this solution with a saying in Spanish to the effect of "Strike while the iron is hot": *El que espera, desespera* — He who waits, despairs.

It was uproarious, raucous fun. The newlywed husbands egged each other on, the brides giggled and chimed in, the drivers split their sides laughing, and Joyce and I played along as I tried to bat back joke for joke. When the bus finally returned to deposit Joyce and me to the Bariloche town center, the *mieleros* (honeymooners) were hanging out the windows wishing us happy travels and, along with the two drivers, blowing us kisses. We blew kisses back, wishing them a lifetime of happiness, and waved goodbye until the bus turned the corner into their future.

For us, the future was twenty-six hours on the dawn bus to Buenos Aires, and it was time again to pack.

8

The Buenos Aires Blues

The honeymoon glow of Bariloche faded, and our trip turned rocky when we arrived in Buenos Aires. Joyce and I had been making friends easily and often along the way and rarely dined alone even when staying in hotels. We connected with the families of my grad school *compañeros* (most from Latin America), we were invited to the homes of bus drivers and travel agents, we followed up leads from one town to the next, and we met other foreign travelers, on a few occasions even running into them again one or two countries away. We were road-savvy but receptive, knowing that the most memorable moments were usually the unexpected encounters.

Buenos Aires, however, while not altogether a bad experience, stopped us short. The city is known as the Paris of South America for its European-style buildings and architecture. Its residents are colloquially called *porteños*, (port dwellers) and in our experience, they were proud and sometimes arrogant. Young men would go to great and aggressive lengths to attract our attention. While we never felt our safety was threatened, we were flummoxed, frustrated, and even a time or two, furious.

Like the evening when two guys persistently pursued us down a street, refusing to heed "*¡Déjennos en paz!*" Seeing that they would not "Leave us in peace" and more fed up than afraid, I suggested we scream. Joyce said, "I've got this," and took the long strap of her shoulder purse in hand, swung the bag around in a wide circle for maximum momentum, and gave one of our sidewalk suitors a breathtaking thump in the solar plexus. Their whistles turned to curses as they disappeared into the shadows, and we walked peacefully to the nearest café.

    I was still in awe of Joyce's bravado the next morning, but she was far from another leap into action and stayed in bed with a sore throat and fever. A doctor's visit to our hotel the following day confirmed strep, and she was confined to bed in our room. I set out to fill her prescription and buy an extravagant bouquet for the mother of a professor from my graduate school days. Dr. Vargas had insisted I look her up while I was in Buenos Aires (BA), and he promised to tell her of my coming on their weekly Sunday phone call. Well, the weeklies went by, and he forgot during each conversation with his mamá to mention my impending appearance. In our last chat before my departure, he swore to me — ¡Te lo juro! — that it would not slip his mind again.

    I climbed the stairs to her stately residence on a leafy, tree-lined street. There was suspicion on her face when she answered the door. Her eyes narrowed as I introduced myself as Susanna, a former student of Roberto's traveling around South America, and surely, he had told her I would be stopping by to meet her. She opened the door and motioned me in, took the flowers without pleasure or comment, and pointed me to a chair. What followed was one of the most unsettling "conversations" of my life. I assumed her son had forgotten his vow to mention my visit, and I tried every tactic to compensate for my surprise appearance and put her at ease.

    Through my small talk about years past as a grad student of Roberto's, life in Northern California, and why I had decided to travel the continent, she watched me intently but offered nary a nod and only spoke to ask clarification of how I'd met her son and how many classes I'd taken from him. When I figured enough time had passed to fulfill my errand as promised, I stood to take my leave, stating out of a sense of misguided obligation that I'd be in BA another week and would call on her again. She responded, *"No es necesario."* I lied that it was a pleasure to meet her and walked back down those stately steps in complete bafflement, but relief that the encounter had ended and another would not be necessary.

The postscript to this weird incident came months later when, back home in California, Roberto begged my forgiveness for having altogether forgotten to tell his mother about the "Susanna" coming to visit. He went on to illuminate why she had been so cold. Before I even spoke my first word on her threshold, she was certain I was the cruel and evil *norteamericana* who had also been a former student of Roberto's with whom he'd been passionately involved and who broke his heart or, as he put it, "She heartlessly dumped me on the trash heap of love." For mamá, this only son was the blameless victim of a vicious vixen, and I, surely the only young American woman and female friend of Roberto's she had ever met, stepped unwittingly onto the stage of her imagination. And to think I'd only agreed to that visit as a favor to him!

It was a lonely time in Buenos Aires. When Joyce felt well enough to step out again, a friendly *porteño*, Ignacio, "invited"[2] us to a fancy restaurant, consumed a pricey wine and the most expensive dish, then rushed off to a "pressing matter," leaving us to pay his bill. No mail from home was waiting for me at the post office general delivery. Nobody in the world knew where I was, and I wondered if the boyfriend even cared. Joyce was still too delicate to travel and, adding to the gloom, the sun refused to shine. It was a cold, damp

---

2 To use the verb *invitar* in Spanish means that you will pay the tab. For example, *"¿Quieres tomar un café? Bueno, vamos—Yo invito."* ("Do you want to go for coffee? Okay, let's go—I'm buying.")

May autumn. Our hand-washed things wouldn't dry, and inflation was so wild that a new pair of socks cost today's equivalent of $42.

Then too, there was the elusive matter of tango. I had read about it, heard the music, and even taught a little of the history about it in my Spanish classes. But I'd never actually seen tango live or been enveloped in the seductive embrace and led through intricate steps with eyes closed and high heels stretching soundlessly behind me. At least, not yet.

I had expected to see marquees, clubs, and studios offering performances and classes, but I hadn't done my homework on the tango of those times. In 1979, not only was neighboring Chile being crushed under the dictatorship of Pinochet, but Argentina was also under the harsh rule of Jorge Rafael Videla and, between repression of tango by the government for subversive lyrics that contained slang and expressed populist ideas, and the Catholic Church condemning the music because the slice of society that danced it was "immoral," tango had once again gone underground.

As in Chile, imprisonment, torture, and *desaparecidos* (people forcibly "disappeared" by the regime) were a terrifying daily reality for anyone perceived of dissent or misbehavior. Many prominent tango figures were in exile or in hiding to avoid being imprisoned or "eliminated." Sadly, in the 1970s and '80s, the evocative musicality and beguiling embrace of tango were also being crushed by the raucous rhythms of American *rocanrol*. For fear of retribution, nobody would be caught dead dancing tango in a club, let alone on a street corner of Buenos Aires, but the music of the moment that blared from storefronts and smoky clubs was the pop rock of *Saturday Night Fever*.

We were *réquete* ready (réh-keh-te: *more* than ready) to leave Argentina. However, yet another setback awaited us. Quite literally, a parting shot.

9

Parting Shot, Falling Missile

This was back in the day when the number of required vaccines to travel in South America would fill two dance cards. We had to postpone a pre-departure typhoid vaccine because it would have conflicted with some other required inoculation we'd already gotten. Now the requisite month had passed, and we had an appointment at the Buenos Aires clinic before getting on a boat that night to cross the wide mouth of the Río de la Plata to Montevideo, the capital city of Uruguay. After we got the required shot of typhoid vaccine, we were passing the time walking through the BA zoo, and I noticed my bag getting heavier with each caged animal we visited. Soon, I started to feel feverish and faint. I turned to Joyce only to see that she was back near the giraffes, sitting on a bench with her head in her hands.

We made it onto the ferry at dusk and accepted a drink in the bar from the two young men from Germany who had helped us with our suitcases as we were boarding. They were ecstatic to find the ferry's bar stocked with Johnnie Walker scotch and were extravagant in buying rounds for the patrons. One was enough for me and Joyce, so off to bed we went. The bunks were roomy enough, but I was restless with fever and Joyce moaned through the night. With the help of our new friends, we got ourselves and our luggage off the ship in the morning and into a hotel. We waved goodbye with the arm we could still raise.

The family of José, my Uruguayan friend in San Francisco, was awaiting our arrival and they were expecting to hear from us. We spent the next two days and nights deeply under the weather. I was unaware of the passage of time, too fevered and dizzy to go out, and sleeping in my shirt because I couldn't raise my arm to pull it off over my head. If this was just a typhoid vaccine, I hated to imagine what a full-blown case would be like. By evening on day two, Joyce felt well enough to leave the room and forage for food, bringing back a to-go box of something forgettable but edible and filling.

On the third morning, I awoke to bright sunshine in a beautiful city, no fever, and enough arm movement to pull off my shirt, shower, and put on fresh clothes. The warm-hearted Méndez family had been worried about our safety and was waiting to meet us. I fell in love with Montevideo, and it became my answer to the oft-asked question, "What was your favorite capital in South America?" In the social and gastronomical whirlwind of visits with José's brothers and sisters and their spouses and kids, we sampled local dishes and spent companionable hours grouped in his mother's living room sipping an Uruguayan favorite drink called *siete y tres*: seven parts red wine with three parts cola—a crazy combo, but it tasted delicious in their company.

After our experiences with the men in Buenos Aires, we took to the streets of Montevideo with four wary eyes and Joyce's hand on the strap of her shoulder purse. When approached by Martín and Arturo, we turned away, but something they said convinced us they really did just want to show two tourists their city. I was still harping about going to a tango performance and finally got to see one that evening after they called a few friends to locate a stage show patronized by old folks and tourists. The performance was underwhelming, but I was satisfied, and we enjoyed the company of Martín and Arturo on the rest of our days in this city. It would be at least two more decades before Argentine tango became the rage with stage shows, nightclubs, lessons, and dance enthusiasts worldwide.

On several evenings of our two-week stay in Montevideo, Joyce and I went to the Manchester Café to order a *cóctel* from our favorite waiter Ricardo. After serving us a gin and tonic, he would return with a very large tray filled with—this will challenge your imagination—fifteen plates of appetizers of amazing variety including tiny slices of pizza, sausage in mustard sauce, little chunks of ham, mini-sandwiches of tomato with pimiento and asparagus, French fries, fried squid, skewered beef on a bed of rice and onions, steamed cauliflower, mussels, garlic toast, pickled vegetables, olives, peanuts, potato chips, and a jelly roll for dessert. This wasn't special treatment for *dos turistas norteamericanas*. It was simply what the Manchester and other cafés in Montevideo served as the accompaniment to a *cóctel*. It all came to about two dollars apiece.

On our last evening in Montevideo, we invited José's sister and her husband to the Manchester since they had offered to drive us to the bus station for departure to Brazil. As we stood up to leave after our meal, Joyce and I gave Ricardo a grateful hug for the camaraderie and warmth he had added to our stay. The red flag signaling "Major Faux Pas" flashed wide in the eyes of Ana and Nelson. They were scandalized that we had fraternized with a waiter and, worse, that we had engaged in an intimate gesture that should be reserved only for family and close friends. How easy it is to commit a cultural blunder in a foreign country doing what one considers normal and fitting back home. I've always tried to be culturally sensitive and appropriate when traveling, but had I known it was unacceptable to hug the help, I would have done so anyway.

I flashed back to my very first trip to Europe as a teen with my

Dutch grandma in 1971. I was pretty bored on a Rhine River cruise with a bunch of other elderly people like her. On day two, I located two girls my age from Los Angeles who were as happy to find me as I was them. Soon we were having impromptu language lessons from the Italian waiters and joining them for evening excursions into town for pub visits on their time off. Grandma knew I was leaving the ship at night—there was never a thought about danger in that safer and gentler era—and I would tiptoe in so as not to wake her when I returned late to our cabin. On the third morning after nocturnal adventures, she was visibly upset with me.

"Grandma, am I coming in too late and disturbing you?"

"No, Susie, but dat mixing with dhe help is something we just dhon't do."

Whoa, I did not see that coming, but I smoothed her ruffled feathers as best I could, and the gals and I kept going out with the Italian boys.

As for cultural blunders on an international scale, U.S. politicians, diplomats, and even presidents who shall go unnamed, have committed major cultural offenses on foreign soil—one assumes for lack of preparation and training by their "handlers." In Islamic cultures, the foot is considered unclean, so the worst thing one can do is cross the leg with the ankle over the other knee (as men often do and at least one U.S. president did) facing the toe and/or sole of the foot toward your eminent host.

Another classic diplomatic faux pas is the American version of a handshake. What do we do when shaking with the right hand to demonstrate additional warmth toward the shakee? We reach out with our left hand to warmly cover the shake. The left hand is considered "unclean" according to Islamic teachings and its use is avoided for eating, drinking, and interpersonal contact. It is the hand used for bathing and for cleaning up after going to the toilet. So, to a Muslim, that simple gesture we think of as showing warmth and inviting friendship can seem disrespectful or even dirty.

I think it's more exhilarating than distressing to know there is a potential cultural faux pas just around the next corner for every world traveler. It keeps us on our toes, sharpens our radar, and makes us want to do our homework in advance!

I carry a cellular memory of how glorious it felt on our first day in Río de Janeiro to shed layers of sweaters and thick damp socks, bask on the beach, and sit in sunny outdoor cafés. We found a cute hotel right in Copacabana, one of the neighborhoods of Rio as are Ipanema, Botafogo and Flamengo. I had given myself a crash course in Portuguese in the thirty-six hours of bus time (1,476 miles) from Montevideo to Rio and was getting by just fine with my version of *Portellano*, as Brazilians gamely called the mash-up of Portuguese and Castellano.

Two linguistic notes about language on the South American continent: 1) I've been told numerous times that speakers of Portuguese (mostly from Portugal and Brazil) can understand Spanish speakers better than the Spanish speakers can understand them, and 2) Early on during our trip, I learned to stop claiming to speak *español* and say instead, "Hablo *castellano*." In the United States, the term "Castilian" refers to the Spanish of Spain, but in South America, *castellano* is simply what they call their Spanish. It has nothing to do with characteristics of the language in Spain, it is simply the term that is used.

Our Copacabana beach friend, Beto, could get by with the basics of ten or twelve languages thanks to his early "education." He'd left his home in Salvador da Bahia at age seven, made his way alone to Rio, lived on the streets, and eked a living as a shoeshine boy, learning bits of languages from his customers as a way to attract business. When we met him, he

Our Copacabana beach friend "Beto"

was in his twenties, no longer a homeless urchin but a college student and aspiring business executive. We treasured Beto as our local friend and guide, and I sometimes wonder where he has taken his life.

One afternoon, the three of us went to the famous Maracanã stadium for the weekly soccer match between two of the highly competitive Rio neighborhoods. This time it was Botafogo facing off against Flamengo. We arrived at the gate and had to declare which team we were rooting for because they were channeling fans in opposite directions to ensure safety and maintain control. I can still see, hear, smell, and feel what happened next, but words will never convey the full impact (pun intended—you'll see) of the experience.

The match is already in progress when we arrive. The stadium is packed well-over its 100,000-person capacity with standing room only. We stand at the upper entrance tiers while Beto scans for seats. We are still standing when suddenly "our" team, Botafogo, scores the first goal. The noise was already deafening with the entire stadium chanting samba and waving huge flags, but now the 50,000+ fans on our side explode into an ecstasy of cheering and screaming. A man in the end seat of a bleacher row several feet above our heads is so overcome with that one-goal advantage that he exuberantly leaps into the air, apparently without a thought as to how that might turn out. He flies briefly skyward until gravity overcomes his heavenly trajectory, and he falls to cement, with me underneath him. He leaps to his feet, still in the throes of an out-of-body experience, hardly missing a beat of screaming adoration for his team. In addition to the flattening impact to my body, my left shoulder is now trampled. I am peeled off the concrete by Beto and Joyce, speechless and bruised, but functionally intact despite the speed and weight of that falling human projectile.

The game ended with a victory for Botafogo. Fans poured into the streets by the thousands in a cacophony of cheering, chanting, honking horns, and screeching brakes—a frenzy that went on all night. I'd heard about soccer mania. I cheered at all my high school and college football games, but nothing had ever prepared me for this. As Beto unforgettably put it, the three things that mattered most to Brazilian men were *samba, ticas* (girls), *e futebol* — in varying order depending on the man.

With the beach scene, the soccer match, the music, the cafés, and everything in between, Rio's sights, smells, sounds, and tastes are forever imprinted with the passion and exuberance that was the essence of my Brazilian experience.

After all this colorful ebullience and the rhythm of samba still throbbing in my veins, I was at first unprepared and then distressed over what awaited us in Paraguay.

10

Potholes in Paraguay

This is eventually to be the tale of why I am a retired teacher in California and not the matriarch of a ruling family of gauchos in northern Argentina, but we have many miles to go before that road forks.

Although I don't recall ever being bored during four months of travel in South America, Paraguay presented a challenge. Asunción in 1979 was the most provincial and dingy capital city on the continent. After bussing in from Río with an overnight stay to marvel at the magnificence of Iguazu Falls, we took turns walking the downtown of Asunción while the other watched the bags in the bus station, searching for a hotel, *any* hotel. After two half-hour tramps apiece, we found a cinder block affair that I noted in my diary as the "hotel" Victoria. I also jotted "shower" and "breakfast," my shorthand to indicate barely tolerable conditions. I mention this less to complain than to segue into the one hundred years that largely explain why even today Paraguay is one of the two poorest countries in South America. (Bolivia comes in first, and we will be traveling there as well.)

In the War of the Triple Alliance (1864-1870) Paraguay fought against the combined forces of Argentina, Brazil, and Uruguay. In perhaps the bloodiest ever conflict on the continent, Paraguay lost over fifty percent of its population of a half million people to battle, starvation, and disease. Of the 221,000 remaining *paraguayos* in 1871, only 28,000 were men, and of those, most were elderly. The economy as well as the army of Paraguay was annihilated, and victorious Argentina, Brazil, and Uruguay annexed huge swaths of its territory into their borders.

By 1932, Paraguay had not nearly risen from this prostration, nor had Bolivia recovered from its near-contiguous series of nineteenth-century wars. As if these two land-locked countries didn't have sufficient economic challenges and disastrous aftermath to deal with, they went to war with each other over the disputed Gran Chaco desert, believed to have rich oil deposits. Though the peace treaty granted Paraguay two-thirds of this territory, the Chaco War cost the country another 3 percent of its population—again, mostly male.

At the time of my visit to Paraguay in 1979, Alfredo Stroessner was in the middle of his thirty-five-year dictatorship, notorious for despotic repression and for harboring Nazi war criminals. Although a local had explained to me that Paraguayan men were treated deferentially because there were still relatively few of them, my jaw still dropped when a young officer in uniform with a sword at his side waited for *me* to open the door for *him*. Despite a certain pallor and worn dreariness about the place, Joyce and I tramped about with good cheer, meeting locals and having pleasant, although not altogether unforgettable, times.

On a day trip to Itauguá, I discovered *ñanduti* (nyan-DOO-tee), exquisite colorful lace woven with needles in circular patterns. That evening back in Asunción, for the first time I heard the sounds of the Paraguayan harp rendering folk tunes of the indigenous Guaraní people. These two wonders of the Paraguayan world—both richly worth a Google—revealed themselves during our brief visit, and months later I carried them home to California, the lace and the music becoming a part of my Spanish lessons like so many other of the continent's memories and mementos.

Our next destination was to be Bolivia, not to further study the ravages of war, but because we were on a trajectory that started in Chile and went through Argentina, Uruguay, Brazil, and Paraguay, and now we anticipated a long but direct bus ride northwest into Bolivia. I had checked and double-checked my *South American Handbook* and saw what looked like a route but was baffled that I couldn't find anything in the "Getting from here to there" section. Map in hand, we went to the bus station for answers.

"See? It says right there on the map: the Trans-Chaco Highway to the Bolivian border," and I traced the line with my finger while the agent shook his head.

"*Sí, señorita, pero no hay autobuses. No está pavimentado.*"

"What do you mean there's no bus service on that highway? We've been on dozens of buses traveling unpaved roads! And I don't want to go back south into Argentina. That's way out of our way, and besides . . . waaaaa!"

Bolivia should have been a straight shot northwest from Paraguay. How could there not be a road suitable for bus travel between the two countries? As I fumed in the Asunción bus station, the ticketing agent unsympathetically repeated the bad news about the route to our next destination: *"No se puede"* — It can't be done. I was indignant over the underdeveloped state of public transportation that would force us to go miles away to the southwest, and incensed because I really did not want to go back to Argentina.

I don't recall if Joyce shook me, slapped me, or delivered a hard elbow thrust into my rib, but I shut up, paid for my ticket to Salta, Argentina, and we returned to the "hotel" to "shower" and pack for early departure after "breakfast" the next day. Though not exactly in a state of equanimous acceptance, I was penitent and apologized to Joyce for my behavior and my patterned reaction of indignance when things didn't go the way they were "supposed to" according to my rules. I wish I could say this lesson produced a permanent behavioral change in my life, but I am still a work in progress.

That evening at the Café El Mesón we met with our Paraguayan acquaintances, had an ample meal, and sang songs in Spanish with them late into the night. It was a sweet and satisfying end to the week of *altibajos* (ups and downs) in Paraguay. In the morning Joyce and I said a sleepy *adiós* to the shabby Victoria and dragged our suitcases down the street to the dilapidated bus depot, destination Argentina—again. I harbored lingering resentments toward Roberto's mother and toward Argentine men in general (at least those of Buenos Aires) as I boarded the bus with Joyce, clinging to my futile resistance against this unacceptable lack of options.

11

Reimagining Argentina: Resurrecting Gauchos

Twenty-three hours after leaving Asunción, Paraguay, we checked into the Residencial Vienna in Salta, exhausted but anxious to get Argentine pesos at a bank or a *casa de cambio* — a currency exchange office. *¡Imposible!* for it was the weekend and they were all closed. How did anyone ever manage in the days before ATM, internet, and international cell phones?

Who knew that these wonderful future inventions awaited us with the promise of easy money anywhere, immediate information about anything in the universe, and relatives, friends, and business associates assuming accessibility to everyone into the farthest reaches of nowhere. In the days before twenty-first century tracking and communication devices, by the time my letter arrived to tell my family where I "was," I could be two or three countries away. It was just the reality of the times, but unplugged travel can be lonely, and I was awed by the isolation of no one in the world knowing where I was and often wondered if my boyfriend even cared.

Unpredictable access to local currency was immensely harder to deal with than no phone calls to home. Cash couldn't be gotten in advance, and we always made this task our first priority when arriving in a new country. As had already happened so many times with banks and *cambios* closed for weekends, holidays, military coups, and electrical outages, in Salta we were sent by the manager of the Vienna up the street to the tourist office, and from there to a nearby lawyer who might buy Paraguayan *guaraníes* in exchange for Argentine *pesos*. He couldn't help us and offered no leads.

Back on the street, we had the good fortune to run into our jolly, burly bus driver who recognized us immediately given that we'd just spent a whole day and night on his bus, and we two *norteamericanas* did stick out in a crowd. He didn't have a solution to our money problems, but he invited us to his house for lunch. We accepted without hesitation because in those days there was simply more trust and connection than fear and suspicion. We ambled up the street with this amiable man and sat down to a big afternoon meal with his wife and kids. We returned, well fed but still peso-less, to the tourist office and the new agent at the desk suggested we ask at the Hotel California just down the street. Mission finally accomplished and a second motive that day for singing "Gracias a la vida", the hotel manager accepted $40 in travelers check and handed us the fair amount in pesos which would tide us over until this brief and unwanted detour to Salta was over.

It was June 16, a cloudy and drizzly afternoon in the early autumn of far northern Argentina. Salta was not someplace we had remotely planned to visit, but here we were for lack of a passable road from Paraguay to Bolivia, and I was still chagrined at this detour south back into Argentina. Joyce, of course, continued to operate from a place of equanimity I hadn't visited yet. She was of a mind to make the best of the setback, so I gamely took a look around. This small provincial capital seemed attractive enough: a sleepy downtown with cafés and shops tucked under the low arches around the plaza. But what was there to *do* here? We pondered this at an outdoor table on the square while sipping *yerba mate* from a small gourd through a sieved silver straw called a *bombilla*. A quick glance into my *South American Handbook* confirmed there wasn't much, though I was intrigued to learn that this was the heart of Argentine gaucho country.

I had read some nineteenth-century gaucho literature in graduate school, but professors and Argentine friends alike claimed that, like the cowboys of the Old West, the gauchos and their culture had largely vanished in modern times. This "fact" had always filled me with a strange nostalgia for something I'd never known but only brushed up against in a few essays and verses of poetry. I concluded I wouldn't see a gaucho in my lifetime unless I went to one of those commercial *estancias* (ranches) for a hokey show where they dress up in the traditional garb, swing bola balls over their heads, and sing for the tourists.

Energized by yerba mate's caffeine, Joyce and I hiked east out of town to see the Güemes monument: the requisite stone pedestal holding an exhausted-looking bronze horse with the victorious hero astride, his hand shading his eyes as he surveyed the distance, suggesting a vision of the entire continent free of Spanish dominion.

A contemporary of the legendary liberators Simón Bolívar and José de San Martín, Juan Martín Miguel de Güemes (1785-1821) organized the gauchos of northern Argentina to fight for independence against the armies of Spain. What his troops lacked in uniforms and training was overcome by the fact that they were expert riders and fierce warriors tempered by the hard life of the pampa and driven by proud individualism that refused to accept the yoke of European rule. Güemes led battles against the Royalist troops from 1815 until his death on June 17, 1821. Gazing up at his statue, I thought I heard the neighing of horses in the distance and, as if on cue, Joyce and I both turned to look down the path into the surrounding trees but saw nothing.

Back at the town square, we were having dinner at the Restaurante El Quijote and chatting with the waiter. His animation went into high gear when I mentioned we'd visited the *Monumento a Güemes.*

"You are returning tonight." It was not a question, more like an order.

"It's already dark. I don't think we'll go back."

"Ah, but you must, for it is the eve of his memorial. The gauchos, they will come." His eyes glittered with the excitement of this major revelation.

"*¿De veras?* — Really? Who will be there? What will happen?"

"You did not come for the 17th of June? You are here just by fortunate accident?"

"*Sí, pues, ehmmm . . ..*" Joyce caught on and ducked her head in fear of where I might take the conversation after my hemming and hawing. I picked up her cue and decided not to tell the sorry saga about my dissatisfaction with the state of transportation between Paraguay and Bolivia. Our waiter threw back his shoulders in a burst of joy at discovering this duo of neophytes at the exact right place and time, and pride at his role in initiating us into something extraordinary.

"Just go. You will be safe. You will see." His smile held mystery and insistence with no further detail.

12

Reimagining Argentina: Walking Among Legends

There were no lights in the park around the Güemes monument and only a few lanterns, but many bonfires burned bright. Joyce and I stumbled along the path as our eyes adjusted to flashing flames against darkness. Around each bonfire were groups of men, playing guitar, singing softly, smoking, and talking to their *compatriotas* in tones of long-awaited reunion. More gauchos kept arriving in trucks with horse trailers and others, to my amazement, were coming in on horseback. I wanted to keep quiet and just observe because I knew we looked out of place—two young women in trench coats with light brown hair and big shoulder bags—but I couldn't contain myself.

"*Buenas noches. ¿Cómo están? ¿Qué distancia han cabalgado?*"

— Good evening. How are you? How far have you ridden?

"*¿Yo? Cincuenta kilómetros, pero mi compadre, casi cien. Nos hemos encontrado a medio camino.*"— Me? Fifty kilometers, but my compadre, almost a hundred. We met along the way.

They left their horses, with saddlebags, bedrolls and all, near dozens of others grazing contentedly under the trees.

Joyce and I continued to stroll in awe, listening to the strumming of guitars and catching snatches of lyrics. We were greeted by many: friendly demeanors, flashing eyes, cups of wine raised in our direction as a reassuring gesture of welcome. I was walking among the real, live, legendary gauchos of northern Argentina! I could hardly believe my fortune to have been transported here by a bolt of grace, undeserving—what with all my whining and complaining—but in an ecstatic state of wonder and gratitude.

There was nothing modern about this scene except for the pickup trucks and horse trailers. Recalling the history of the gaucho campaigns against Spanish rule under the leadership of Güemes in Salta, the scene in the park that night could have been the gathering of victorious guerrilla gauchos after they routed the royalist troops in the 1817 Battle of Humahuaca.

I looked intently at these men gathered to honor their war hero 178 years after his death, men whose ancestors had suffered persecution, fought wars, and lived off a harsh land for centuries. We were feeling more at ease among the gauchos and less hesitant to draw closer to the bonfires. I noticed that most of them were dressed alike. Many wore *bombachas*, the bloomer pants, tucked into black leather boots, and some sported the traditional felt flat-brimmed hat, but almost all were wrapped in a blood-red poncho trimmed with black fringe in honor of their martyred hero.

Joyce and I spoke to each other only sporadically. I was in a place beyond thought, time, and words. How is it this gringa could resonate profoundly with a people and their history that she had never shared? My reverie bubble suddenly popped when a handsome young man advanced from the shadows and declared, "*Me llamo Roberto Marcelo, y quiero que me saquen la foto con dos bellas rubias europeas.*" That stopped us in our tracks and woke me from my trance. I fumbled for a response to "I am Roberto Marcelo, and I want my picture taken with two beautiful European blondes."

"*Bueno, pues, somos norteamericanas, de California. Susanna y Joyce, mucho gusto.*" I decided to leave it at "pleased to meet you" and forgo the discussion of how we aren't really blondes except in

Latin American countries where most people have very dark brown hair and eyes, and somewhat darker complexions.

A bystander took his camera and snapped the photo for Robeto Marcelo who then walked on with us while speaking passionately of the regional patriotism of the Salteño people; the importance of the annual memorial to Güemes; the gaucho dress and customs; the provincial *presidente de los gauchos de Güemes, el señor* Campos; and the parade and other celebratory events taking place tomorrow on the 17th of June. Joyce and I were now completely in the moment and in for the full ride of what-could-possibly-happen-next.

We repaired to an impromptu café at the edge of the park for a glass of wine and a tasty supper of tamales and *locro*, a stew of squash, meat, and hominy. Roberto Marcelo was no less enthusiastic upon learning we were American and not European. He proposed a trip into town, and with just a quick exchange of approving looks, Joyce and I agreed to go. We squeezed into the bench seat of his pickup truck (a major player later in this story) and he drove us to his office where he regaled us with cookies from one brother's factory, chocolates from another's, cigarettes, sweet cakes, and greeting cards.

Quite miraculously in the time before cell phones or text messaging, his best friend, Rudecindo Campos, showed up at the office door. The son of the president of Los Gauchos de Güemes of the Argentine province of Salta was still wearing his dark red poncho trimmed with black fringe. We admired it as the finest of all we'd seen, talked about our experience in the park, took coffee with them in a café on the plaza, and agreed to being driven around the night city to see, among other sites, what they claimed was the tallest church tower in South America. We talked about gaucho life and the music of Argentine folk singer-songwriters Jorge Cafrune and Atahualpa Yupanqui. After years of studying the cultures and customs of South America, it was all coming alive along this long road around the continent, and most magically in this unanticipated encounter with the gauchos.

When they dropped us at our hotel that night, Marcelo and Rudecindo instructed us as to exactly where to position ourselves the next morning for the best view of the gaucho parade. It was late and we still had to pack because we had already bought bus tickets to Bolivia for the next day. (Yes, there *was* a paved and passable highway directly north.) In the morning, we taxied to the station to leave our luggage and then walked back to watch the parade. Despite the muddy route, it was a colorful and inspiring display of gaucho pride in their history and culture, and of devotion to the memory of Güemes.

Unlike at the gathering in the park the previous night, here the women, *las gauchas,* had a co-starring role. The matrons looked to have stepped in from the nineteenth-century prairie in ankle-length, long-sleeved, high-necked pastel cotton dresses, riding sidesaddle abreast of the men, who wore the flared *bombacha* pants tucked into high boots and the dramatic red poncho of the gauchos of

A gaucho couple preparing to join the parade

Güemes. The men's horses all sported the traditional *guardamonte*, the billowed stiff leather "wings" attached to both sides of the saddle to protect the legs of the rider and the flanks of the horse from the brambly undergrowth of the pampa called *maleza*.

The chilly breeze wafted wood smoke mixed with scents of muddy horse manure and leather. From where we stood, we could see each pair of flag-bearing riders come around the corner directly in front of a huge red and white 7Up billboard, the only visual proof that this actually was the twentieth century. There were only a few onlookers besides Joyce and me because it seemed all of Salta was astride a horse riding in patriotic reverence. Then, ebullient Rudecindo, who family and friends called "*El Negro*", rode around the corner beside the 7Up billboard, spotted us and yelled, "*¡acá, acá!*" to make sure we saw him "here, here!"

The parade was memorable, but our most intimate experience of the gauchos was yet to come as all four of us piled into the front seat of Negro's truck to head for the Campos family ranch, the largest *estancia* of the region.

13

A Fork in the Road

We four bounced in the front seat of Negro's pickup through the town of Salta and out to the Campos family's estancia, the ranch of the ruling gaucho family of the province of Salta. Luckily, our bus for Bolivia didn't leave until early evening and we had several hours to spend with Roberto Marcelo, Rudecindo, and the Campos family members, who were just arriving home from riding in the parade.

You might wonder why Rudecindo was nicknamed "El Negro." In Spanish-speaking cultures, this is a common and endearing *sobrenombre* (nickname) for the darker-complexioned child in the family. There is also the nickname *güero*, with the feminine form *güera*, for one who has lighter skin. A man might affectionately call his wife *mi negrita*, or perhaps *mi gordita* (my chubby) or *mi viejita* (my old woman). She might call him *negro/negrito, gordo,* or *mi viejo.* There are two lines in the famous Mexican song "La Llorona" that say, "*Todos me dicen 'El Negro,' Llorona, negro pero cariñoso / Yo soy como el chile verde, Llorona, picante pero sabroso.*" — "Everyone calls me 'El Negro,' Llorona, dark-skinned but affectionate / I'm like the green chile pepper, Llorona, spicy hot, but tasty" — Provocative lyrics, ¿no?

Sure enough, when the four of us arrived at the estancia and Joyce and I met Rudecindo's brothers, he was obviously the darkest as well as the youngest and best looking of the three. We sat in big wicker chairs on the wide veranda with cousins Miriám and Eugenia,

Marcelo, Negro, and his two brothers. The one I can still picture clearly also had a memorable *sobrenombre*. Édgardo was known as Pelado (Baldy) to his family and friends.

When I told Édgardo how enthralled I was to stumble upon the gaucho culture still thriving in northern Argentina, he swelled with pride that this heritage had held strongly into modern times. He explained how he went to his office in a business suit every morning to be a lawyer in town, then returned to the estancia by early afternoon, changed into working gaucho garb, saddled his horse, and worked the ranch until twilight. He said it was the "city" way to have a professional day job but dedicate more than half one's time to the gaucho life. Perhaps this lifestyle was typical for landowners of the upper class, but most of the thousands of remaining Argentine gauchos were ranchers and laborers working full-time at herding cattle and sheep and training wild horses.

Édgardo looked wise with his big round spectacles, and elegant in a fine gaucho suit of light gray wool *bombachas* (loose-fitting trousers) tucked into high black boots, and matching jacket with a black wool scarf tied around his shoulders. Lively conversation continued as he he prepared the *mate*.

Yerba mate (mate herb) has become a popular tea in the U.S. but in Argentina and Uruguay, also in Paraguay and southern Brazil, it is an essential part of life. Its preparation and consumption are a daily ritual that brings family, friends and co-workers together for communal sips and conversation, whether in a gathering on the veranda, a morning family kitchen, or a break in herding horses at a muddy river crossing. In the Buenos Aires airport several years ago there were few paper coffee cups in hand, for most Argentines had a metal thermos of mate tucked in a briefcase or under the arm. The dry mate

Edgardo Campos on the veranda passing the mate

leaves are steeped in a small calabash gourd of the same name (*mate*, pronounced MA-te) that has been prepared especially for this use: dried, "seasoned," fitted with a base, and perhaps decorated with a bit of silver or carving. As the friends and family sit companionably together, the gourd is passed from hand to hand and each takes a sip from the *bombilla*, a straw with a sieved bulb at the end usually made from silver or stainless steel. Hot water is added to the gourd as needed

El mate y la bombilla

and the camaraderie continues. People may take mate together several times a day as a refresher (about half the caffeine as coffee), but more essentially as a symbol of friendship and a way of sharing companionable times over conversation with family and friends.

It was an honor to be sipping mate with this extraordinary family of gauchos on their ranch house veranda, all gathered in living memory of Güemes, their nineteenth-century liberating hero. The distinguished family patriarch, Señor Campos, arrived from the festivities in town and joined us in the mate circle. On the road in front of the house, many gauchos traveling home in trucks or on horseback waved and tipped their hats to *el presidente y su familia* as they passed. For the long ride home, most of them surely carried a pouch of coca leaves in addition to their thermos of mate. Marcelo had told us of how he would ride twenty-four hours at a stretch herding animals over hills and pampas (flat grasslands) with just the poncho for warmth, mate for strength, and coca leaves *para quitar el hambre* — to take away the hunger.

Yes, coca is a basic ingredient of cocaine, but to it are added kerosene or diesel fuel, sulfuric acid, caustic soda, and potassium permanganate to make the drug. In Ecuador, when my travel/study groups took the *teleférico* (tram) from Quito at 9,350 feet up the Pichincha Volcano to 13,000 feet, we would sip coca tea in the café at the crest since the unadulterated leaves are famous for warding off not only hunger but altitude sickness. The tea was mild and grassy-tasting with no dramatic effect.

Marcelo and Rudecindo gave us a tour of the rustically elegant house and the family photo gallery. Then they took us out to the corrals to meet the horses and impress us with a demonstration of the skills every gaucho learns in boyhood with a leather whip, a long tapered pole, and *boleadoras* or *bolas*, a cord with three leather-covered rocks on the ends, used to take down running animals.

Too soon, it was time to think about getting to the bus terminal in Salta. Back at the ranch house, we gathered for a group picture with Marcelo, Rudecindo, and the cousins. In the photo, Joyce with the Scandinavian features and blue eyes looks exotically European, but I could pass for a member of the family, smiling dark-eyed from beneath the flat black brim of Miriám's loaned hat. We said goodbye to cousins and siblings, and to Señor and Señora Campos, and drove with Marcelo and Rudecindo back into town. With time to spare, we stopped at Marcelo's office where he gifted us more cookies, a calendar with images of the Salta town and province, and to me, a small booklet of early twentieth-century vintage that I treasure as a relic and an extraordinary memento: *Los Estatutos y Reglamentos de los Gauchos Tradicionalistas de Güemes* — "The Statutes and Rules of the Traditionalist Gauchos of Güemes."

L to R: Rudecindo, cousin, cousin, cousin, Miriám, Joyce, Susanna, and Marcelo

Low on gas, they left Rudecindo's truck at the office and we took Marcelo's to the bus station. Since it was still a bit early and we had a long road ahead to Bolivia, they invited us to the cafeteria for sandwiches, but when we returned to the terminal, the bus had already left! In my journal I wrote, "Everyone ran around in all directions for a few minutes, then we threw the luggage into the back of the truck and roared off down the road after the bus." When we came to a fork in the road, Marcelo skidded the truck to an abrupt stop in the middle of the rural intersection where one route became two. They knew the terrain (gauchos are legendary trackers), but the bus could have taken either route to eventually arrive at the Bolivian border.

Baseball legend Yogi Berra, in giving directions, famously said, "When you come to a fork in the road, take it." That's exactly what we would have to do, but *which* fork was to be a coin toss of a decision. I was conflicted with mixed feelings, and I knew Joyce was too. We wanted to continue our continental adventure but wished we could stay at least another day or two with the gauchos. I've often asked myself, why didn't I say, "Turn back"? It's not like we had an appointment to keep over the border in Bolivia. Was I unwilling to waste a bus ticket on our tight budget, or did I opt for the unknown of a new country over the unknown of being drawn deeper into the spell of a captivating foreign culture? Was I afraid to complicate life too far out of my control?

Marcelo looked at us quizzically. Joyce shrugged. I closed my eyes and pointed. He revved the engine, and we veered to the right in a cloud of dust. Against the better part of my hope, we overtook the bus and sped on ahead of it to the police road station. Marcelo told us not to speak *castellano*, but to play the two innocent *norteamericanas* who had missed the bus. The police threw up a makeshift roadblock, and when the bus caught up to us, we said quick goodbyes to our gaucho escorts, to the most culturally romantic and exciting experience I'd ever had, and to my nagging feeling that maybe this time I shouldn't run away.

We waved from the back of the bus, they waved back, then Marcelo turned the truck and drove away on that decisive fork. The sticker on the back of his tailgate read, *"Argentina, amor mío; Argentina por toda la vida"* — Argentina, my love; Argentina for all my life.

14

Under the Southern Cross

In the dead of night, the bus from Argentina to Bolivia stopped in its snowy tracks. Joyce and I were jammed tight in our seats because, in the first place, they were made for the average Bolivian stature and size, and secondly, we were wearing nearly every garment that had accompanied us on this trip around the continent. I was sitting on my hands to keep them warm and had put a satchel over my feet. I couldn't stop thinking about life without toes if I lost them to frostbite. One hour, two hours . . . we waited, and wondered. The driver and another man left the bus a few times, but we couldn't see what they were doing outside. Passengers were mostly quiet, some snored despite the fearsome cold. When one of them returned after talking with the driver, the rumor of frozen gasoline drifted in icy phrases from the front to the back of the bus. Despite that unlikely diagnosis, we mysteriously got underway again and, three hours later, the sun rose over distant mountains to light up the barren *altiplano* (high plateau) dusted with snow.

The Bolivian Plateau is the second largest in the world, bested only by the high plateau of Tibet. This *altiplano* of relatively flat land inside the central Andes and between high volcanic peaks has an average altitude of over 12,000 feet—it literally takes your breath away! The legendary volcanoes soar at 20,000 feet or higher. There are 196 volcanoes in South America between Colombia in the north and Tierra del Fuego at the southern tip of the continent. On a map, the continent's western flank looks like an almost uninterrupted lineup of diamond-shaped dominoes. Almost a third of them fringe the altiplano of western Bolivia, southern Peru, and northern Chile and Argentina. This high plain is harsh, rocky, and barren, but I found it beautiful for its jagged outcroppings, and the haunt of endless winds across dry earth. The distant volcanoes seemed to float impossibly on the horizon like mirages in a brutally cold desert.

As soon as we got off the bus in Villazón, we sought out the marketplace for wool sweaters and thick socks. We ate a quick meal of hot stew, then bought our tickets for the twenty-hour train to Oruro deep into the altiplano, deciding to spring for first class at $8.40 because we were sorely in need of rest and a bit of comfort. The ride started off beautifully with llamas grazing a meager meal on the sere ground as the landscape became gradually more mountainous. The other gradual change was the number of people in our first-class train car. Joyce and I had been ecstatic about having a whole car to ourselves and had taken all our damp socks and undies out of the bags and hung them on the back of the empty seats.

At first, we thought it an anomaly that a few more people took seats in "our" car, and we giggled our embarrassment while quickly gathering the laundry. As dusk turned to night, the train made many stops to pick up more passengers. The overhead lights didn't work, and newcomers were stumbling through total darkness. There were no more available seats in "first class," and there was no heat either. By 1:00 a.m., so many people filled the aisles and covered the floors that no one bothered searching for a seat anymore. A young couple with beseeching eyes tucked their baby basket at my feet. A man had already commandeered the armrest of my aisle seat with apologies, and spent the night there. All was enveloped in darkness, but I could hear women with babies, and parents temporarily separated from children and luggage and reunited in the confusion of passengers seeking somewhere to settle. Did the train have a restroom? Pointless to wonder for we could never have navigated there anyway.

The cold was as terrible as that of our experience last night on the stranded bus—surprising given this many bodies sardined together. I was again assailed with worries of frostbite resulting in absent toes and fingers. We were bundled in our clothes, sweaters, and trench coats, but every Bolivian was wrapped in a thick wool blanket. It was an essential garment they wouldn't dream of traveling without, while we Americans, on the other hand, just assumed there would be heat on the train.

Despite the shared experience somewhere on the continuum between discomfort and suffering, no one objected, argued, or raised a voice. People who live in this harsh land *aguantan la privación* — they put up with hardship. Every so often, I would hear a murmur, "*Qué duro es viajar*"— How hard it is to travel, and occasionally a disembodied voice admitted fretfully, "*Qué frío hace*" — It's so cold. A little boy across from me wriggled around wide-eyed but silent while his parents slept huddled into each other. The stars in the clear black sky were the most magnificent I had ever seen. As Joyce slept soundly, I reached across to put my fingertips against the frozen window and touch the four points of the Southern Cross, the iconic constellation "Crux" visible year around in the Southern Hemisphere.

With the first rays of sun over the mountains' crest, the frost on the *inside* of the train car windows began to melt. With sunlight waxing and my body beginning to thaw, I pulled out my *South American Handbook* and began to read up on Bolivia. The history, peoples, customs, food, and attractions of the country that we were about to enter warmed me with anticipation and enthusiasm.

A young policeman who had boarded at dusk, stretched his arms and back after spending the night standing next to the drafty door. In the new light, he tiptoed among the passengers to make sure everyone was okay. The man who had spent the night on my armrest struck up conversation. Conrado was a teacher specializing in curriculum planning who had just spent a year at the University of Colombia getting a degree in Administration. A woman across the aisle and the young policeman, Àngel Flores of the drafty door, joined the conversation and recommended sites to see in La Paz and regional Bolivian specialties to sample. Ángel wanted to be the first to introduce us to Bolivian folkloric music and produced from inside his jacket a rustic musical instrument called a *zampoña* consisting of a double set of hollow reeds tied together by a hand-woven ribbon. After playing a melody, he handed it to me saying with sweet formality, "*Se la obsequio.*" — I gift it to you. I practiced the traditional Andean song he taught me under the bright eyes and alert ears of the other passengers. As I was playing the song, we were passing the marshy expanse of Lake Poopó, and Joyce was shooting photos of acres of flamingoes taking flight in flashes of pink, black, and white.

La zampoña gifted to me by Ángel Flores

Some of us got off the train in the small and thoroughly indigenous town of Oruro. Passengers still aboard en route to La Paz passed our bags out the window, while passing *into* the windows were steaming bowls of stew and bags of toasted fava beans from the vendors at the station. As we were saying goodbyes and good wishes to our companions of that dark and frigid night, Ángel wouldn't let Joyce take our picture until he took off his wool sweater and cap, smoothed out the police uniform shirt, and put on his tie. Fear of frostbite was long forgotten as we waved goodbye to the warm smiles and kind eyes looking down upon us from the windows of the train.

Susanna and Ángel Flores in his police uniform

After two nights of traumatic cold on the altiplano, the icy thin air of Oruro sparkled with sunlight. Gazing at miles of jagged terrain extending to distant Andean peaks, I breathed a familiar sense of oneness with desolate landscapes and anticipated what this strange new land would reveal.

At home in a desolate landscape

15

Bolivia: The Gathering Storm

I've often pondered the wheel in wonderment that such an essential tool for the movement of heavy objects had to actually be "invented"—that the fashioning of something round popped like a lightbulb into a 3,500 B.C. brain; that ancient peoples used their forehead, crown, and back for transporting goods; and that in the year 1,000,000 B.C., Fred found no other option than his feet for propulsion of the Flintstone family car—though it *did* have wheels!

There we were, headed for yet another bus station, lugging two large suitcases that had grown heavier with each country we'd traversed. We hadn't brought excessive clothing, but we *had* packed for the climate variables of an entire continent. Now we were carting gifts purchased and received, and mementos from every destination. From Chile, I had the book of Pablo Neruda poetry and delicate flowers woven from brightly dyed horsehair, mate gourds from Argentina, a leather bag from Uruguay, a bikini from Rio de Janeiro (weightless, and space-friendly), *ñanduti* lace and ceramic cups from Paraguay, and those bulky alpaca woolens bought upon arrival in Bolivia. I was reducing some of my consumables every day: lotion, vitamins, chewing gum, and the wheat bran I had to explain in great embarrassing detail to officials at every border crossing. Still, I was acquiring far more than I was divesting.

Back to the invention of the wheel: Shopping for luggage in Sacramento back in March, we bought what turned out to be the precursor of the rolling bag. We each had one large, soft-sided suitcase with the standard sturdy top handle and the "high-tech" breakthrough of four tiny wheels underneath with a small metal ring on the side to attach a flimsy, plastic leash. The advertisement showed a petite woman in a short skirt and high heels effortlessly dashing her obedient case through the airport by its leash with her left hand while waving to a handsome pilot with her right.

In the first place, the revolutionary wheels were small and rickety while the cases were wide and tall. The second factor was the condition of most streets and sidewalks in South America. I was lucky to even *have* a suitcase after it crashed over onto its side yet again, this time in the middle of the street, and a car appearing suddenly from around the corner narrowly missed running it down. Still clinging to the leash of the downed beast, I might have been swept away with it had the car not swerved off in time. That was the end of the dream of rolling luggage. From then on, we ditched the useless leashes and just dragged the behemoths by the handle.

After one night in Oruro, we lugged the luggage (lug: Middle English *luggen*, to pull) aboard a bus with the help of a willing local and set off on the relatively short hop of three and a half hours to La Paz. Across the high plain of the Andes, the little villages of low mud-brick houses contrasted with views of towering Mount Illimani (21,122 feet) at the edge of the *altiplano.* At each brief rural stop, village women reached up to sell fruit and bread through the windows before the bus ambled off to the next outpost. After passing a small herd of llamas grazing on sparse vegetation, we turned a corner and suddenly had our first view of La Paz: a wide bowlful of civilization shimmering in the distance.

As the bus wound down the sides of this bowl, past shacks with tin roofs held down by rocks, a fellow traveler explained that the poorer people lived at the higher levels where the air was thinnest at over 13,000 feet, and foot travel meant plying muscle-burning, steep, narrow streets. More well-off folks lived in the depth of the bowl (about 12,000 feet) where the terrain was easier to negotiate. That was also where the hotels, agencies, museums, marketplaces, shops, and cafés were to be found.

Altitude sickness is called *soroche* (soh-ROH-chay) and its effects range from uncomfortable to debilitating, and from dangerous to deadly. Visitors to La Paz, the highest capital city in the world, are well advised to sit down to an occasional cup of coca leaf tea to acclimatize and lessen the effects of soroche.

Although it is the third largest producer of natural gas in South America (behind Argentina and Peru), Bolivia was and still is the poorest country on the continent for several reasons, though a dearth of natural resources is not one of them. In addition to natural gas, there are 238 minerals in Bolivia with major mining extractions of zinc, tin, silver, gold and lead.

During the nineteenth and early twentieth centuries the country was involved in several wars, one of the most disastrous being the War of the Pacific (1879-1883) against Chile. Vanquished Bolivia not only had suffered thousands of casualties but was obliged to cede its entire 240 miles of coastline to Chile, bringing that country's stretch of Pacific to four thousand miles. Bolivia became land-locked, cut off from the commerce and trade benefits of having access to the sea.

One hundred years later, Joyce and I just happened to arrive on the centennial of that fateful war, and had we not boned up on local history we would have thought Bolivia had been forced into the terms of the treaty just last year, so ominous was the militancy of the proclamations. While neighboring Chile was blasting fireworks to celebrate this auspicious anniversary of its victory and the economic benefits of an extended coastline, Bolivia was militantly mourning its *litoral cautivo* — captive coast. There were signs and banners everywhere proclaiming, *"Bolivia es un país litoral"* — Bolivia is a coastal country, and *"Antofagasta es y será nuestro"* — (The now-Chilean city of) Antofagasta is and will be ours.

During its 140 years of being land-locked, Bolivia has continually sought to regain its status as a littoral country and, at the very least, obtain an easement of sorts for commercial access through Chilean territory to the Pacific Ocean. In October of 2018, the highest court of the United Nations dashed those hopes. In response to Bolivia's appeal for judges to order Chile to enter negotiations with Bolivia for access to the ocean, the U.N. International Court of Justice voted 12-3 that Chile has no legal obligation. And thus, the country declined to negotiate.

Bolivia is a deeply indigenous country with 62 percent of the population belonging to thirty-seven native groups—the largest being Aymara and Quechua—and a brutal history of politically and economically disruptive military coups. Well-planned social and economic programs are doomed to failure when the government abruptly changes every year or so. When we were there in 1979, Bolivia had already experienced 150 *golpes de estado* (coups d'état) in its 154 years of independence from Spain in 1825. At this present writing, there have been 190. In addition to militant claims for the lost coastline, the second ominous sign of unrest in that late June of our visit was the widespread rumor that the presidential election in less than a week would precipitate another military coup.

A third ominous sign of what might come occurred as we were about to emerge through the big glass doors of our otherwise modest hotel for our first foray into La Paz after a long, restorative nap. At the desk, there was a message for Joyce addressed to *La bella rubia escandinava* — The blond Scandinavian beauty — with a very formal request: *Puedo hacer su correspondencia?* — May I make your acquaintance? When we opened the doors to leave the hotel, two young men lounging on the steps jumped to their feet and asked for *una consulta*, literally "a consultation," but we were sure they weren't looking for advice. We parried their advance and, taking a deep breath of thin cold air, launched our exploration of a city that, for Joyce, was to be life changing.

16

Luck and Love in La Paz

As if rumors of an impending military coup, militant proclamations that the coastline "stolen" by Chile in the War of the Pacific would be re-taken by Bolivia, and eager men lounging on our doorstep were not ominous signs enough, there were more. On our first day wandering the streets of La Paz, Joyce and I stumbled upon a market shaded by tarps from the piercing sun. (Remember that in the world's highest capital city, we were 12,000 feet closer to our star than at sea level.) There were tiny stalls with indigenous women selling what few vegetables could be grown at such high altitude, baskets and pots, colorful alpaca shawls, and eek!—a string of tiny desiccated horses.

The Quechuan señora eyed me as I edged in for a closer look at what I later discovered were llama fetuses. My mind recoiled and my stomach churned. I took a step back but couldn't turn away. It was callous of me to take a photo; she protected her spirit by covering her face. Surrounding the macabre display were vials and jars of creepy contents. Shakespeare's lines from the witches' scene in *Macbeth* roiled through my head precisely as I was thinking I might lose my breakfast on the cobblestones of what we later found out was *La Calle de las Brujas* — The Street of the Witches:

"Eye of newt, and toe of frog,
Wool of bat, and tongue of dog,
Adder's fork, and blind-worm's sting,
Lizard's leg, and owlet's wing,—
For a charm of powerful trouble,
Like a hell-broth boil and bubble.
Double, double toil and trouble;
Fire burn, and caldron bubble."

On La Calle de las Brujas—The Street of the Witches

I saw no boiling cauldrons, but my mind was full of questions and frustration for the internet had not yet been invented, and my *South American Handbook* did not inform that the llama fetus was one of the most important elements in the offerings to Pachamama, the goddess Mother Earth. This deity has a tremendous following in Bolivia: indigenous people burn offerings of coca leaves, food, and drink to Pachamama as a ritual of gratitude, respect, and reverence. A kindly Swiss woman who'd taken up residence in La Paz picked up on our confusion and shed some light on what was before our eyes. Thus, I learned that in one of those jars was powdered dog's tongue to be secretly added to a man's food to make him loyal to his lover like a dog is to its master. She also informed us that the dangling desiccated frogs held the promise of good luck for their new master.

I wonder if twenty-first century travelers armed with internet at the touch of a cell phone or tablet would meet even a fraction of the people that we did as we stumbled our way around late twentieth century South America. How to find train schedules and bus routes? What about road conditions? How to solve the mystery of llama fetuses festooned around the market stall, find the right potion to inspire fidelity in a mate, or relieve the effects of soroche? Why were the potatoes purple and black in Bolivia, and what in the world was that fruit we were yet to meet in Peru that looked like a green hand grenade? The only way to answer these questions was to talk to people—locals, expats, fellow travelers. Along with all our countless inquiries, we made memorable warm acquaintances while listening to their gracious answers, this savvy Swiss ex-pat being just one of legions.

For my purchase in the marketplace, I chose Ekeko, the grinning god of abundance and prosperity with a fat cigar between his lips and all manner of worldly goods in his embrace and strapped to his back: currency, diplomas, toys, a can of Coca-Cola, overflowing pots, and brimming baskets of food. Ekeko was small and light, my finances were dwindling so I could use some abundance, and my unwieldy suitcase didn't need any more bulk or weight. Counting on Ekeko to deliver, I passed on the lucky frog legs, but I might have tried the power of powdered dog's tongue had Kevin's dinner plate been in range.

Another "sign" more odd than ominous was the omnipresence of calendars and posters with semi-nude women in provocative poses in every restaurant, store, and agency. The first sighting was at the customs office back in Villazón on the Bolivian border coming in from Argentina. I thought it unusual in a government installation but couldn't have guessed that it was to manifest as a national obsession. What a strange contrast to see all these square feet of flashy female flesh papering walls in one glance and, in the next, Quechua and Aymara women in the street covered from toe to head in wool knee socks, multiple flaring wool skirts, blouses, and shawls, their heads topped with the ubiquitous derby-type hat favored by indigenous *bolivianas*. It looked to me like a single Quechuan woman could wear more layered articles of clothing for an outing to market than the total packed in my over-stuffed suitcase. Was this cold-climate coverage the inspiration for the craze of papering public walls with images of semi-nude women?

Indigenous Bolivian women

Somewhere between llama fetuses and girlie posters—I think it was at a show of Bolivian folk music and dance at Los Escudos—we met Alejandro and his entourage. He was in his early thirties, tall, handsome, and gainfully employed in a high-level position with a ministry of the Bolivian government. In those days, anyone with economic or political power was of predominantly Spanish, and not indigenous, blood. That meant they were taller, whiter, usually more schooled, wealthier, and part of the valued minority that ran the country. Alejandro fit this profile but, to his credit, was working to improve the indigenous lot and bemoaned that these populations were forever stuck on the harsh *altiplano* because there was no infrastructure or transportation in the warmer geography of eastern Bolivia in the Amazon basin. When queried, he grudgingly acknowledged they wouldn't leave the frozen high plain anyway because that's all they and centuries of ancestors before them had ever known.

There is no denying it: this first meeting was love at first sight. Alejandro was starry-eyed and Joyce glowed in his presence. He was articulate, charming, well-traveled, worldly, and romantic. On their first date, he brought her a perfect white rose. To me, since I was to tag along as their chaperone, he presented a red one. I believe we drove up to the top of the bowl to see the lights of La Paz below. I remember without a doubt, however, where we ended up. Late in the evening, the city hospital opened its doors and Alejandro and I half-carried Joyce inside. She was doubled over, clutching her gut, blood dripping from her nose. Soroche . . . and serious.

Whether it was by medication, infatuation, the motivation of only thirty-six more hours in La Paz, or a combination of all, Joyce recovered enough to spend all of those hours with Alejandro. I agreed to make myself scarce and go out the next evening with his sidekick, Coco—not coincidentally rhyming with "loco." An erratic young man with a big appetite for whiskey.

The Casa Blanca nightclub was packed. Coco and I squeezed into a tiny table in the corner of the upper room. Several yards in front of us was a four-foot balustrade separating the dance floor below from our seating area. After Coco's third whiskey, I had firm doubts that the evening would be pleasantly memorable, but what happened next was so unexpected, followed by my cartoonish escape, that it lives in memory as a comically unforgettable "date night" with tinges of compassion, but no regret.

17

Escape from Casa Blanca

Joyce +1 and Susanna +1—both of us in a long-term relationship, both with conflicted feelings about our boyfriends, though for different reasons. I wanted fidelity, communication, and at least some thoughts about our future, but Kevin had had his dalliances and wasn't dependable. Joyce wanted a loving partner for travel, adventure, and exploration, but her guy wanted a safe, quiet homebody existence. Though I hadn't had a letter from my lover in weeks, I wasn't looking for a replacement.

While I was happy for Joyce and Alejandro off somewhere finding new love, I was less than ecstatic about being jammed into a dark corner of the Casa Blanca club with Coco "El Loco" now on his fourth whiskey as I nursed my glass of wine. First, he professed his undying love (it was our second meeting), and then he offered me everything he "owned": I forget how many houses, acres of ranch land, head of cattle, silver mines, planes, and millions in cash. He swore if I left for Peru the next day as planned, he would track me to California and bring me back to Bolivia to marry him. All he asked was that I love his little daughter from a previous marriage. That was touching, but I told him it just wouldn't work, exaggerating that I was already engaged to the boyfriend back home. Another whiskey. Now he was becoming angry. He grabbed and clung to my arm, but my distress was immediately replaced by joy when a miracle happened: he passed out on my shoulder.

Tucked between the two walls of a tight corner, we were hemmed in across the front by tables packed with patrons. Coco was dead weight on my left side. I tried to wake him, hoping it wouldn't work. As he slipped into a crescendo of snores, I wrote my farewell on a cocktail napkin (kind of like ending a relationship by text or tweet these days), slipped it into his shirt pocket, then scanned the forty-five degrees before me for a possible escape route.

I settled Coco's weight against the wall, stood up, and squiggled out around the table. I took a deep breath and then launched into the jungle of tables and chairs with *con permiso* (excuse me) at every step. Reaching the discotheque entrance was impossible, so I made for the four-foot barrier separating our upper-level tables from the dance floor below. Swallowing pride and embarrassment (*¡Loca turista!*) and thankful for long legs, I climbed over it and dropped down several feet to the edge of the crowded dance floor. With more *con permiso* and *mil disculpas* (a thousand pardons) I dodged through dozens of embracing couples and finally found a door that said *Salida* (Exit).

Stars shone bright in a cold freedom sky, but I didn't know how to navigate by them and hadn't a clue how to proceed toward our hotel. This wasn't the first time I was turned around and disoriented with no idea which way was north, and no mental image of the lay of the land. On these travels in South America at age twenty-nine, I was daily discovering new aspects of just how very directionally challenged I was and to this day continue to be. This has occasioned endless unintended adventures, especially as I went on to lead groups to foreign places for study/travel programs, experiences that deserve a volume all their own. Suffice to say for now that, if left to my own directional devices, I will pore over a street map for an eternity and then always take a wrong turn.

I was in awe of Joyce's fully functional internal GPS and unfailing sense of direction. Typically, we would enter a city in the dark on a bus that did several loop-de-loops and maneuvers in reverse before parking in the station. Then we would walk (dragging those stupid suitcases) around numerous blocks to find adequate lodging. In the morning and to my amazement, she could point in the direction from which we had arrived and retrace not only our steps but the bus's meanderings as well. This seemed an incomprehensible ability, as unfathomable as shape-shifting or astral projection. It was also what leveled our field and made us symbiotic traveling companions with different specialties to contribute and clear reasons to value the other's skills.

As desperately as Joyce wanted to be fluent in Spanish, join in conversations easily, and take the lead in explaining to customs officials why they really needn't cut open our gift bags of coffee beans, her language skills weren't up to it, though they were improving notably along our journey. Here on the road, decisions, negotiations, reservations, clarifications, and explanations had to be made at every turn, and it was inevitable that I would lead almost all of those communications. Joyce may not have thought her orientational forte was as valuable as my language skills, but as I've always said, if she hadn't been there telling me which way to turn, I might still be wandering the continent.

There was one instance when both my Spanish and her sense of direction failed. It was somewhere in Bolivia before we got to La Paz (to where we'll be returning in a moment). We had to change buses to reach the destination, so we bought the ticket and found a café for a meal. At departure time, I had a verbal exchange with an official that prompted me to load us onto bus B heading south. We were relieved and relaxed to be cocooned into two soft seats with nobody sitting on our laps, thinking about a long nighttime nap, our eyes drooping toward sleep. Suddenly, Joyce's GPS kicked in and she said, "Whoa! I think we're going the wrong way!" You've got to be kidding. I *so* wanted to sleep! I got up from my seat and humbly asked the driver where we were going—back to the dumpy town whence we'd come. Both of us felt chastised: I, linguistically and Joyce, directionally, although she quite redeemed herself by calling it after only forty miles of mistaken road.

After my clumsy, dramatic escape from the La Paz discotheque, I was still taking deep breaths of night air outside the Casa Blanca with little sympathy for Coco's eventual awakening to abandonment and a hefty bar bill, though I was asking myself, where *is* my hotel. Taxi to the rescue and I was delivered in fifteen minutes for about seventy-five cents. Given my *trastorno* (upset), I would have paid many times that fee to complete my escape from Coco and the Casa Blanca.

Once locked into the hotel room, I threw my beat-up suitcase on the bed and started to pack for tomorrow's departure for Peru. It didn't surprise me that Joyce was still out with Alejandro, and I wondered what to do if she opted to stay with him a few more days or forever. Peru was waiting for me. Cusco and Machu Picchu were calling my name. I kept stuffing my suitcase.

18

Skewered Hearts and Tourist Stew

I couldn't have extricated myself from this next misadventure without Joyce's help. It's a good thing she decided to bid goodbye to Mr. Tall, Dark, and Handsome in Bolivia and get on the 8:00 a.m. bus with me northbound to Peru. We pulled into Cusco at 7:00 the next morning after lunch and dinner stops in Copacabana and Puno where we shared tables and conversations with other travelers.

During the sleepless night, the absence of interior lights in the bus precluded reading and Joyce was in no mood to talk, so I wound out a long fantasy about returning to Northern California and opening a Montevideo-style café that served the full table of small-plate delicacies with each cocktail order. In the cafés we had frequented a month earlier in the Uruguayan capital, over a dozen little plates were served as the complimentary accompaniment to the order of a cocktail or a glass of wine. It was an enticing culinary reverie, but, in an American market, nowhere near cost-effective.

When I left on this South American odyssey three months earlier, I had five years of restaurant experience behind me with ten more still in my future. However, food service was not my career but rather a way to support my Spanish teaching habit. Hospitality was year-round, whereas teaching was freelance assignments at various colleges tacked together but interrupted by weekends, holidays, and the three-month summer break. I never did open the Café Montevideo in Sacramento, but foreign foods in substance and style are still fodder for my fantasies.

Now once again, we were in a new country experiencing a completely different culture, and while it was the same language, Peruvian-accented Spanish sounded distinct from what we had heard in Bolivia. Despite lack of sleep, I was in a state of high excitement, and I was famished. The Hotel Portales seemed adequate and clean, so we stashed our things in the room, and I set out to explore, and to eat! My *South American Handbook* provided ample detail on national foods, and I always arrived in new places with my own scribbled "menu" of the regional specialties I intended to sample.

At the top of my list for Peru was *anticuchos*. My Italian mamma used to feed us some pretty unusual things when we were little kids, like raw clams, liver paté, chicken gizzards, and the stomach lining of a cow, so I didn't hesitate to order beef heart chunked and grilled on a skewer. Joyce didn't join me in the adventure, for her mind still lingered in La Paz, her heart was hurting, and her appetite was depressed.

I raved about the anticuchos to the waiter at the Café Adriana as he brought me a second serving, but he warned me not to partake of them from the numerous street stands, claiming that some vendors were skewering heart of dog and not beef. *¡Qué asco!* — Yuck! This curbed my enthusiasm for becoming the Cusco connoisseur of anticuchos, and I limited my samplings to the tables of reputable cafés.

We planned to see a folklore show of music and dance that early evening, so a return to the Portales for a shower and nap was the next order of the day. I badly needed a hair-washing! With my mane eight inches below my waist, washing it was a monumental project and, in foreign travel, sometimes an impossibility. We always checked the bathrooms while looking for hotels to ensure there was hot water. Why hadn't we verified this before checking into the Portales?! We gathered up our things and quickly switched to the nearby Hotel Qorikancha.

I ditched my siesta, but we made it to the folklore show on time, I with my damp hair clipped into a big knot atop my head. Evening temperatures drop fast at 11,152 feet, and we were wearing layers topped with sweaters and our trench coats and, of course, we had our ever-present shoulder bags tucked at our side. I always kept mine short-strapped and firmly against my ribs between my armpit and waist. Perhaps you are thinking, "Hmm . . . all these boring details. Could there be a method to this monotony?"

We were walking back to the hotel after dark and came upon what looked to be a street party. We circled around the edge of a tightly packed crowd of about eighty people, all enthusiastically cheering because the object of their attention was a pyrotechnic display the likes of which I had never seen before and will never witness again due to the probability of an increase in the lawyer population and subsequent liability lawsuits. It lives indelibly in my memory for its colorful weirdness, for the element of flaming danger and, of course, for the aftermath.

Joyce and I edged closer to the backs of the people crowded before us, trying to be unobtrusive, and yet still get a look at what was going on in front of this pulsating mass of Peruvians. Flames were flashing and we caught the acrid smell of burning wood before we could make out the details. Luckily, we were at least a head taller than most Quechuans and we focused our eyes on the two men facing the press of people, now announcing their second act. Each held a long pole with a large, rickety wooden construction attached to the end: an airplane on one, a ship on the other. The "pilot" of the airplane had lit the tail on fire and, as flames spread through the structure, propellers began spinning, rockets were firing, and small pieces of moving parts—tinder turned to cinder—flew off, further stoking the excitement of the audience.

Then, the "captain" of the ship put a match to the hull and made the flaming frigate "sail" toward the onlookers, spewing parts of stern and prow, shooting "cannon balls," with pieces of the masts sparking as they fell to the ground. The crowd was stirred into a frenzy by the time they brought out the last pole from which hung the grand finale for the fireworks show: a four-foot effigy of a man with lanky splintered-wood limbs. There was raucous laughter as everyone noticed the outsized protrusion from its crotch. The touch of flame started the chain reaction from one flailing body part to the next. The 180 degrees of humanity, with these two curious *norteamericanas* bringing up the rear, pressed together even tighter. When the "male member" caught fire, hoots of delight filled the night air. With heat and ingenious engineering, the crotch assemblage began a 360-degree spin, faster with every rotation.

Suddenly, a flaming piece of penis the size of a barbecue briquette broke off and sailed toward the throng. Like a school of fish moving in unison, the whole mass gasped and jerked violently away from the projectile. The momentum of bodies was like a sudden poke to a lineup of dominoes, except that no one fell down, except Joyce and me: she onto hard ground, and I backward into a huge pot of thick soup overseen by a Quechuan woman planning to sell to a hungry crowd after the pyrotechnic event.

I was in shock with soup up to my armpits. I must have flailed when I went down, because those armpits were the only thing that kept me from immersing neck-deep into that colossal pot of potage. Joyce was on her feet before I even registered what had happened (something about a flying penis?), and grabbing me by the lapels of my trench coat, gave me enough momentum to get my hands onto the sides of the metal cauldron to help her hoist me out and upright. I steadied myself, gooey and shaken, but not injured.

"My clothes are ruined, but I'm lucky to be out of that mess," or so I thought while turning toward Joyce who was looking ominously over my shoulder.

19

Tug-of-War over Tourist Soup

The soup lady charged in from behind me, gripped my left arm with one hand and my purse-clutched-against-ribs with the other, and demanded restitution for the lost earnings of the servings of soup ruined by the unfortunate juxtaposition of my backside with her pot on that fateful evening in Cusco.

Coming to my rescue again, Joyce latched onto my right arm, and the tug-of-war began. The Peruvian woman was no taller than my shoulder, but she was stout and strong. She was wrenching my left arm and clawing at my purse with all her strength while I clutched it to my side with all of mine. Joyce was simultaneously pulling me to the right and trying to defend my purse. Meanwhile, I had not given up on diplomacy, logic, and sincere apology: "*Ay, señora, lo siento tanto.*" — Oh, ma'am, I am so very sorry. "*Mil disculpas le ruego.*" — A thousand pardons I beg of you. I stuttered words of defense: *back of the crowd, flying piece of carbon, knocked backward* . . . She was unmoved and not even listening. It was my purse for her soup—no discussion, for this was business, not theatrics. Ironically, had she not grabbed me, screamed for payment, and gone for blood, I would have given her every *sol* in my wallet to compensate for my accidental ruination of her pot of soup.

Now onlookers were beginning to take sides as two other diminutive women joined her and the Quechuan chorus screaming for my purse crescendoed. A kindly older man joined forces with Joyce and me and suggested that the women back off, but they held their ground and their claim on my purse. Despite Joyce's stalwart stand at my right, my soupy legs felt like jello, my arms were going weak, and I was beginning to lose hope of surviving this tug-of-war with purse and person intact.

Suddenly, heaven opened up, and two angels in the earthly form of Peruvian policemen appeared and ordered the Quechuan women, "¡*Cállense y suéltenla!*" It took more than one authoritative command and some manhandling of the soup lady's fingers to get them to obey the official command to "Pipe down and release her!" *Los policías* asked for both sides of the story and conceded that the offended soup vendor could begin. She claimed I had aimed my derriere into her soup pot with diabolical intention. My turn after hers, and by then I was in such a hysteric state that what threatened to burst forth was a coin toss between hyena laughter and blubbering tears. It took a huge effort to gain enough composure to recount the crazy pyrotechnics, the flaming projectile, the backward surge of the crowd, and the last domino crashing backward into the soup pot. I had to keep this as serious and simple as possible, for had I said, "flying piece of penis", my hysteria would have exploded into hyena, and I would have lost my few sympathizers in the crowd and credibility with the only two people who could release me from this mess.

And release me they did, while trying to get the soup lady to accept the unacceptable: that it had been an accident, no intentional damage but, yes, a misfortune for the large amount of capital and potential income lost as a result. The two police held off the irate woman, stopped me from opening my purse to pay her something, and shooed Joyce and me down the street. Their order was firm but friendly, with more than a flicker of humor in their eyes: ¡*Váyanse!* ¡*Váyanse!* ¡*A su hotel ahora mismo!* — Go! Go! To your hotel right now!

Joyce and I hooked arms to steady ourselves, pressed our purses securely between us, and sped down a long block of wordless and breathless power walking, never glancing back or even lifting our eyes from the ground. Joyce navigated a turn to the right, another half block, and we finally looked at each other, broke stride, and almost collapsed onto the sidewalk from laughter as we took it all in: the crazy fireworks, the tug-of-war, and our soiled and soupy trench coats and pants. My newly washed hair, all pinned up, remained unsullied, but I was souped to my underwear. And Joyce? How did she get soup with stewed meat and vegetables down the side of *her* trench coat and into *her* socks? As we relived the event and recalled that she had fallen down alongside the soup pot, I considered how much liquid I had displaced while descending at great speed into that enormous vat, and how a soupy tsunami must have gushed at an angle that sullied her quite effectively as well.

You might wonder, how did we not get burned? The soup had been heated elsewhere, and the pot placed on the ground behind us was ready to serve. I don't have a scientific answer, but our trench coats were sturdy and by the time soup reached socks and shoes it must have cooled in the night air to an innocuous temperature. More to the point, I was in such hot water by then that some *sopa caliente* seeping into my socks wouldn't even have registered as a concern in that critical moment.

Still feeling rather unhinged and being a few blocks yet from our hotel, we spun out a scenario of how the purveyor of the tainted soup could have made an extra profit had she parlayed the setback into a wacky benefit for the hungry crowd, though for that she would have needed a sense of humor that, in our brief exchange, did not manifest: "Come one, come all! My soup has a secret ingredient that, although you have just witnessed it disappear into the night, has left behind its mysterious essence in the sweep of a trench coat, a splash of magic, a blessing from Mama Quilla, Quechuan goddess of the moon and defender of women. Think of the possibilities! This elixir could add six inches to your height, materialize a fat purse at your side, and ensure an exotic foreign trip in your future. Why, right here, in this very pot . . . !"

Tensions released as Joyce and I stumbled back to safe haven at our hotel, still shedding chunks of potatoes and onion. My hysteria subsided as we skipped dinner to celebrate our narrow escape by starting the process of hand-laundering a mountain of soupy clothes.

20

Making Our Way to Machu Picchu

Whenever I talk with someone who's been to Peru, I am always curious as to exactly how they "did" Machu Picchu. I've never come across anyone who arrived, toured, or exited this mysterious icon of Incan civilization quite the way Joyce and I did; and nowadays with predetermined routes, time limits, and the daily visitor cap extended to 5,600, no one ever will.

Some did the legendary four-day hike on the Inca Trail over the mountains and into Machu Picchu from above. It used to be that you didn't need a permit or a guide, but now one must apply in advance and hire a trekking agency. The majority of visitors take the tourist train from Cusco to arrive at the town of Aguas Calientes around midday, then a shuttle up forty minutes of steep switchbacks to the Inca citadel in the sky. They then examine the amazing system of terraces and stroll the ancient stone structures on predetermined routes with a horde of other tourists, making it impossible to get an unpeopled view of the site's magnificence, and surely drowning out the whispered echoes of a civilization that was about to be annihilated by Francisco Pizarro and his Spanish soldiers in the mid-1500s. Joyce and I created our own low-budget agenda, which resulted in a more adventurous and infinitely more private experience. In fact, for the duration of our visit, we practically had Machu Picchu all to ourselves.

Thanks to those two young policemen, I still had my purse after last night's soup pot caper, though our trench coats were still damp from handwashing in the sink. We were again low on cash and in need of a local bank to change traveler's checks. You wouldn't believe how many bank holidays there are in the South American calendar—about as many as there are major Catholic saints' days. This was the feast of Saints Peter and Paul, and it wasn't the first time we were in need of cash with all the banks closed. To make matters worse, El Banco de la Nación, the only bank that changed foreign currency and traveler's checks, was on strike.

After a cheap meal of shrimp chowder called *chupe*, we bought fruit, bread, and water in the Cusco marketplace. I tamped down my new phobia of short, stocky indigenous women to buy a little bag of coca leaves from one of the dozens of vendors selling from enormous bushels at every stand. I didn't realize I'd made an illegal purchase until I saw a policeman strolling between the stalls batting a nightstick against his palm as the women in his path hastily scooted their bushels under the cloths covering their table of wares. The policeman kept his head high, and his eyes averted from the women scurrying to hide the piles of coca leaves.

As we were leaving the marketplace, I was craning my neck for other law enforcement when I picked up the scent of slaughter and realized we were treading on glops of fresh blood on the street. A quick check of our position suggested we were skirting the live animal market, confirmed by the sight of an old woman walking a few yards in front of us with two sheep heads fresh from slaughter grasped by their horns swinging at her sides.

Sucking on a cheekful of coca leaves isn't about getting high. In the Andean countries of South America, it's a buffer against cold, hunger, pain, fatigue, and altitude sickness, especially if one adds a chalky substance to help extract the juices from the leaves. Coca is also a remedy for headaches, toothaches, indigestion, sore throat, muscle aches, and arthritis. Chewing coca leaves and drinking coca tea are ancient customs in this part of the world and provide far less stimulation than a cup of coffee, black tea, or yerba mate. I was saving my leaves for the early morning ascent to maximize my cultural experience of Machu Picchu. They would also help me handle the altitude and the physical challenge of what was to be an almost sleepless night.

The crowded local train leaving Cusco that afternoon was redolent of sweat and hot cooked food, full of tired children and lively chickens, and devoid of tourists. Before we pulled out of the station at 2:30 p.m., vendors made their last sales of bean and popcorn tostados, corn husks stuffed with vegetables, *chicha* beer (made from chewed corn and spit), and *chicha morada* (from purple corn and pineapple, no spit). After six very culturally authentic hours of smells, sights, and sounds, we arrived at 8:30 p.m. in Aguas Calientes where we would spend the night and depart early to ascend the remaining 1,300 feet of Machu Picchu's 8,000.

Aguas Calientes in 1979, gateway to Machu Picchu

It was dark in Aguas Calientes. There was no electricity, and we were literally feeling our way along the walls. The two lodgings mentioned in the *South American Handbook* had no vacancy. Someone pointed us toward a dorm room, and we groped our way further down the main street buildings to reserve two of the dozen cots for an exorbitant six dollars apiece. At the town's only operating café, we shared a meal with Richard, a Kris Kristofferson look-alike from Texas, while owner don Pepe gave us instructions for our early morning foray into the sky.

Through the short night in the communal room, a baby cried, two children coughed, and an Argentine man with that unmistakable accent discoursed loudly. Strange dreams of jungly mountains and dark corridors floated through my semi-consciousness. We dozed in our clothes until pre-dawn, then tiptoed past the cots and started walking up the railroad tracks with Richard to catch the first shuttle for the trail of switchbacks to the top of Machu Picchu. As the minibus got underway with just seven of us travelers, I pinched off the stems and inserted the coca leaves against the inside of my cheek one by one, then added a bit of *lejía*, an alkaloid made from ash. I sucked on the juices and pondered history and mystery as our little bus made the slow ascent from the Urubamba River to the still-invisible summit.

The magnificent Incan empire was already weakened by civil war when Pizarro and a band of 168 Spaniards began a forty-year siege of destruction, recruiting large numbers of native allies who hoped to end Inca domination over their peoples and lands. Machu Picchu was built in 1450, less than one hundred years before the fall of the Inca Empire in 1532. The function of this mountain top city has long been studied and debated, and many archaeologists believe it was constructed as a retreat for the Incan emperor Pachacuti and his nobles, though some theorize it was a religious site or a military outpost. The grounds contained many human skeletons thought to be the remains of workers who lived and died in the service of royalty. John Verano, anthropologist at Tulane University in New Orleans, commented, "If you thought of Machu Picchu as a royal hotel . . . for the Inca emperor and his guests, then these were the staff who cooked the food, grew the crops, and cleaned the place."

We were almost to the top just minutes before dawn when it became startlingly clear why Machu Picchu, one of the Seven New Wonders of the World, had remained undiscovered until the twentieth century.

21

Magnificent Machu Picchu

When the caretaker arrived with his huge key on that early morning of June 30, 1979, Joyce and I were the first to walk through the gates of Machu Picchu, followed by Richard and the other four passengers from the minibus. Everyone chose a different path through silence profound as a prayer. Morning mist blurred the

Switchbacks up the mountain from Aguas Calientes to Machu Picchu

landscape above and below while ancient stones emerged from the foggy swirl as clouds shifted to make way for the day's sun. What *was* totally clear on that early morning was why Machu Picchu had remained hidden from the world until the early twentieth century.

When we were ascending those switchbacks in the shuttle bus, I strained my eyes toward the summit at every sharp turn to catch my first view of the old stones. My excitement was running incredibly high, and it had nothing to do with the coca leaves tucked inside my cheek. I had taught about this legendary site in college classrooms for years and now was about to see it for the first long-awaited time.

Joyce's magnificent photo of Machu Picchu
with Huayna Picchu in the background

Nothing... nothing... still nothing. I could see the top of the loaf-shaped mountain, but it wasn't until the last switchback that the mysterious stones of the abandoned city came into view and Machu Picchu revealed its breathtaking splendor. Rumors had circulated for centuries about hidden cities of the Incas. When local farmers led American explorer Hiram Bingham to the site on July 24, 1911, it was mostly covered by dense vegetation. However, he soon realized he had come upon the fabled city the Spanish *conquistadores* and everyone else had searched for but failed to find for four hundred years. To the few indigenous people living at the site and farming the terraced mountainside, this meant nothing, but Bingham holds credit for what many consider the greatest archaeological discovery of the twentieth century.

I wandered up to the famous sundial carved in granite past walls of beautifully hewn and fitted stones, many of them monolithic. How did the Incas build the largest empire of pre-Columbian America with no system of writing and only rudimentary tools? And how in the name of the sun god *Inti* did they manage to construct this complex city in the steep terrain of a mountain top, through dense vegetation and without draft animals, out of huge stones quarried far below, precisely cut and smoothed to fit one another and survive centuries with no mortar? Some of the stones weighed more than fifty tons, and they fit together so perfectly that not even a needle can be inserted between them.

Machu Picchu is the prime example of the style of masonry called Dry Ashlar, a construction technique that does not use mortar to bind the blocks together. It must have taken hundreds of men to push even one stone up the mountain and lift it into place, a feat I've never been able to imagine. One understands that it is not just for its beauty that Machu Picchu is named as one of the seven New Wonders of the World.

We spent several hours roaming the site from early dawn to late morning. Sometimes our paths crossed and Joyce and I read to each other from the guidebook, but mostly I walked alone in awe and silence, tuned in to fleeting voices of a lost age. Machu Picchu belonged to me, to the remnant echoes of its ancient people, and to the resident llamas who grazed placidly nearby as I munched on oranges and nut bars.

Communing with the resident llamas of Machu Picchu

Reluctantly returning to present time, I found Joyce and we pondered the steep steps of Huayna Picchu (young peak), the mountain that towers over Machu Picchu (old peak) in the classic photo. The trail up Huayna Picchu is called "the stairs of death," fearfully precarious, though very rarely living up to its name. There are still many things you can do in Latin America that, if there were more liability lawyers, would be totally out of bounds, but the Huayna Picchu trail is still open and in use. These days, you have to pre-register to climb it, but even now there are no handrails and only a few safety lines.

Joyce, Richard, and I started the rocky ascent into open sky. It was steep and narrow, slippery with moss and moisture from the morning mist. We went about a third of the way up, high enough to revel in views of the stone ruins and terraced slopes below. That was a sufficient dose of danger for one morning, and we turned to assess the difficult descent. But something else was sending a chill down my spine and raising the hairs at the back of my neck. We were high enough to get a clear view of what was just starting up the steep switchbacks from the Urubamba River at the base of the mountain.

The tourist train had pulled into the station at Aguas Calientes, and a couple hundred invaders were piled into shuttles making their way up the switchbacks to our private Shangri-La. Knowing that the minutes of our incomparable experience were numbered, we turned back down the treacherous steps of Huayna Picchu. With our feet planted firmly on the welcoming earth of "old peak," we sprinted across the walled courtyards and around the massive stone structures toward the edge of the mountain.

Richard had come in on the Inca Trail and had lived between Aguas Calientes and the summit for nearly a month already. He knew the terrain and was leading the way. All we could think of was getting out of there before this army of tourists arrived to defile our magical experience. As the first of several minibuses disgorged its contents of plaid shorts, Hawaiian shirts, safari hats, and swinging cameras at the gate, I launched straight down the steep slope behind Richard and alongside Joyce through dense shrubs, muddy terrain, and scrubby trees. We slid, we skidded, some places we actually "hiked," and we laughed with pure joy at this utterly spontaneous and totally essential act.

Since all the tourists were now up in Machu Picchu, we took advantage of the peace and quiet of Aguas Calientes to experience just that: "hot waters" from the natural springs to sooth our bumps and scrapes from that wild descent. We passed a delightfully restorative couple of hours in the hot springs with Richard and two British travelers, Rupert and David. Before boarding the train back to Cusco, we spent the rest of our meager cash on stuffed potatoes, chocolate, and *granadilla* (passion fruit). We said goodbye to Richard, who would stay to commune with the stones and spirits of Machu Picchu for another month or so.

David and Rupert were on the train with us, and after bearing their criticism that we were rushing around the continent too fast, we settled into friendly observations about constellations (Southern Cross and Scorpio), Spanish grammar, and the legendary stones of the nearby Incan sites of Sacsayhuamán and Hatunrumiyoc. Joyce and I did not think we were traveling the continent too fast. We still had two days in Cusco to visit other Incan wonders and see the sights before our next looong bus ride. We two agreed that we'd never make another visit to Machu Picchu because nothing could equal, let alone surpass, the magnificence of today's. In five subsequent trips to South America, I have never gone back.

In Sacasayhuamán, struck speechless by stones

We prepared to press on, not in haste, but with the urgency of excitement for the next new adventure. The inexplicable presence of massive, enigmatic drawings in the desert was magnetizing us westward toward the Nazca plain. We would soon find out why we could not resist their pull.

22

Follow That Trench Coat

Even though our general trajectory was north toward Lima where we hoped love letters awaited us at general delivery, I had convinced Joyce that it was absolutely necessary to detour southwest for our next destination. On our last night in Cusco, I caught up on notes, wrote a letter to Kevin, and debriefed with Joyce about our recent adventures. Then in the darkness I let my mind wander and ponder late into the night. What if she decided to turn back and join Alejandro in La Paz? I had asked her straight out if she was considering it, but her answer to my query was a noncommittal parry. If she were to exit our travel duo to form a romantic one with him, would I amble on alone? I would truly miss her, but there wasn't a doubt in my mind that I would.

But then again . . . I was thoroughly dependent on Joyce's sharp sense of direction during our many weeks of travel. Hers was the trench coat always in the lead. An inner compass is one of those pieces of human equipment I do not possess—a definite setback in a foreign land, but even quite a challenge close to home. I find malls and department stores especially treacherous. Entering them, I must make careful note of which door I came in. The one between cosmetics and women's shoes, or was it the one at handbags? When exiting a smaller store in a mall, I won't know whether to continue my trajectory by turning right or left unless I've previously

The trench coat I always followed

self-instructed: "When you leave Chico's, turn toward Cinnabon." I avoid malls for this and other reasons.

Since I live in a small city with a main street that runs basically north-south through the middle, I can almost always tell you which way I am pointing. However, though I drove to the college campus every working day for twenty-four years, no matter where I was indoors or out, I could not accurately point a compass direction. I had a vague idea in my head of what was where, but I was always ninety or so degrees off. I learned this while saying to my students things like "*La costa está al oeste*" — The coast is to the west — while erroneously pointing south; *"Mi mamá vive al sur"* — My mom lives to the south — but I was pointing east; *"Voy a Reno este fin de semana"* — I'm going to Reno this weekend — and my mind's eye would have me pointing north instead of east every time. It became a classroom joke as students would laugh and do a group point in another direction, or one would gently move my arm ninety degrees to the right or left, like moving the big hand of a clock.

It seems impossible that I led twenty groups of adults on travel/study programs in Mexico, Ecuador, and Italy. Reader's incredulity is well-founded because, yes, I did spend a lot of time wandering in circles, coming back upon the landmark I thought I had left at least a half mile back. My travelers in Oaxaca, Mexico assumed that while they were in language classes from 9:00 to noon, I must be sleeping in, leisurely reading the news over a *café con leche* (caffe latte), painting my nails, and shopping for souvenirs. In fact, I spent those morning hours plying uneven sidewalks to locate the museums, markets, galleries, churches, and the restaurants that would accommodate fifteen people; calculate the order of arrival; and map out the routes of the walking tours I led every afternoon. Thus, I managed to inspire their confidence as someone who was firmly footed on familiar ground and could navigate them from points A to B for daily series of cultural and culinary adventures.

This strategy worked okay until one afternoon in Oaxaca when we left the Basílica de la Virgen de Soledad, and the light rain turned monsoon. We were just a few blocks from our dinner destination, the Restaurante Catedral, and we sallied forth in a forest of umbrellas moving toward the *zócalo* (main plaza). After twenty minutes of sloshing down streets that had become raging rivers with objects almost the size of Volkswagen Bugs floating by, I was stunned to peer out from under my umbrella at the side entrance of that same Basilica that should have been far behind us. I recognized the stone steps up to the large wooden door, although so much water was pouring off the courtyard, they had become a twelve-foot cascade gushing onto our feet. One of my student's flip flops broke free and joined a flotilla of flotsam roaring down the street.

After a general mutiny, I was relieved of my status as guide for the evening. My traveler friend Mary Anne took over as the lead umbrella and within minutes we arrived at the restaurant dripping and laughing at my folly. The staff herded us into the bathrooms to stash the umbrellas and remove as many articles of wet clothing as possible yet still be presentable in the dining room.

The other end of the orientation spectrum includes people like Joyce who unfailingly know where they are in any place at any moment. Without her guidance, would I be forever meandering South American streets, studying the map and turning my whole body in different directions trying to figure out, "Now, if Calle Victoria is to my right, which way do I turn to get back to the hotel?"

I've always wondered if being directionally challenged is related to my inability to type or play piano without looking at my hands. A friend told me how in her high school typing class she could do 120 words a minute with zero errors. The teacher was in such disbelief, she accused Tammy of cheating, impossible as that would have been. I asked her about her sense of direction, and she reported that it was excellent. I do believe there's a connection.

When I took my nieces to Italy a few years ago, I was a confident tour guide in Rome because, in addition to the dome of St. Peter's, there were always massive arches and monumental obelisks to keep me oriented. In Lucca, I managed okay as long as we kept riding our bicycles on the wide Roman wall that encircles this jewel of a city. But in Siena I was always turned around on its curvy, claustrophobic streets even after five visits—again, leading groups!

Enough of arguing for my limitations because, despite the lack of a GPS, one of my most taken-for-granted gifts is a fully functioning internal gyroscope. Whether on a loop-de-loop roller coaster, in a stunt plane doing snap rolls and barrel rolls over the Napa hills, in the back seat of a car on a winding road with my nose in a book, or sailing high seas in choppy waters, my axis remains stable and I don't get motion queasiness. This is a really good thing, because Joyce is hanging with me as the other half of our adventure duo, and we are headed for the plains of Nazca, about to get into a very small plane.

23

From Pigpen to Paradise

It was 350 miles southwest from Cusco to Nazca, but we were to experience once again how the sum of miles can be meaningless without taking into account the condition of the road. When we boarded the bus in Cusco at 8:30 a.m., I had on a clean shirt and my hair was freshly washed, a big deal considering that it was a yard long from part to thigh, and thick enough to make several wigs. All over South America, water availability, pressure, and temperature were a constant challenge in our budget accommodations. In some places, the water would only be turned on in the rooms for a couple of hours in the morning and at night, and hot was more of a luxury than a given.

On that road to Nazca, as soon as we hit the open highway out of Cusco, our tresses, clothes, face, and lungs were taking on layers of grime through the open windows of the one and only bus that plied this route. There was no air conditioning, it was too hot to travel with closed windows, trucks and buses in front of us were throwing up clouds of dust and dirt, and there were thirty hours still ahead on this hell's highway.

Beyond distressed, I was *indignant*. If they couldn't pave the road, then at least get a bus with AC! The Peruvian passengers were predictably placid in their acceptance of this plight, and Joyce took it with her usual calm, though even she had to raid her equanimity bank to get through it.

To make matters worse—and on a day like this, there had to be *something* to make them worse—my knees were jammed against metal since the distance between seats had been measured to comfortably accommodate the average indigenous femur measuring under twelve inches. The entire road was mountainous and unpaved. Dust soon covered everything and was all I could smell and taste even though I'd dug out a red bandana to tie bandit-style around my face. We tried to use seat time to catch up on our journals, but I gave up on penning a letter after "Dear Mónica and Susanita" alone inked up half the page due to potholes and rocky swerves. I had two treasured *Time* magazines, scoured from kiosks in Cusco, and I read every word, eyeballs bouncing and brain fretting over the oil crisis clutching the U.S. in 1979, which would later contribute to the recession of the early '80s.

There were lots of locals but only three other tourists on the crowded bus, the only ones either naive or crazy enough to do this torturous route from Cusco to Nazca. The locals got off and more came onboard at every stop, filling the aisles for the hour or two ride between villages. On the first day there was a dinner stop, and on the second we filed out for breakfast and again for lunch in rustic roadside eateries, taking a table with a Scottish boy, a girl from New Zealand, and a woman from Australia. The dust was endless, and arriving in Nazca at 4:00 p.m. on day two, we stepped off the bus looking like versions of Pigpen in a *Peanuts* cartoon, emanating clouds of accumulated dirt and debris with every move.

In the main town plaza where the bus let us off, we were eating ice cream from cones to cool our throats and revive our taste buds when a kid introduced himself as Beto, the nickname for Roberto, and offered to carry our luggage to the Nazca Tourist Hotel across the street. We humored him but were doubtful we would be staying at that lovely rambling hacienda with red bougainvillea spilling down adobe walls and doves cooing from the tiled roof. It only happened one other time during our four months in South America (in Oruro, Bolivia at the Hotel Plaza), but here in Nazca, it turned out we *could* afford to stay at the finest place in town for a total of $24 for two people, two nights. The room was airy and spacious, and the grounds were like an oasis in the desert with colorful flowers cascading from baskets and palm trees shading the deck chairs around the pool. We felt like Cinderellas in the fairy tale, though still covered in cinders.

It's not that tourists didn't come to Nazca, but they usually stepped off a twin-engine plane from Lima rather than staggered off the local bus covered in sweat and grime. Celebrating good fortune at a bargain, we showered off the outer layer of dust, then changed into swimsuits and did a few laps to wash away more of the grime before attacking the persistent layers with shampoo for the hair and a sink full of detergent for the clothes. Looking presentable once more, we ventured out to make our debut in the plaza and soon realized we were already quite the local sensation.

The plaza was an extension of the oasis atmosphere with shade trees and inviting outdoor cafés. We soon ran into Beto, the young boy who had hauled our unruly suitcases to the hotel. He introduced us to Cholo, one of the pilots who flew tours over the Nazca Lines in the desert. Those lines were the reason I had insisted to Joyce that we travel through thirty hours of physical, grimy hardship to this remote town so that we could hire a pilot, who just happened to have materialized before us in the shade of the plaza. Was it coincidence or cahoots? I didn't care because things were working out quite nicely.

The ancient Nazca Lines went from relative obscurity to international curiosity and controversy when Erich Von Däniken published *Chariots of the Gods?* in 1968. Von Däniken claimed that many examples of art, architecture, and sculpture from ancient cultures depicted astronauts and spaceships. The first edition of his book is full of grainy photographs to support his theory. He hypothesized that extraterrestrials were welcomed as gods by ancient peoples who developed advanced technologies and religious beliefs based on their influence. Von Däniken makes the case that such monumental earthly artifacts as the pyramids of Egypt, Stonehenge in England, the Moai (monolithic figures) of Easter Island, and the Nazca Lines of Peru were either created by the ancient astronauts themselves or by the humans who learned and applied advanced technologies acquired from them.

Joyce and I took a taxi to the desert airstrip and were greeted by Cholo who regretted that he was already booked to fly some Americans from Pennsylvania on a tour of the Lines. Luckily, his fellow pilot Solón was available and soon the three of us were airborne in a single-engine plane over the flat desert with the first full drawings coming into view.

Boarding with Solon

It is widely accepted that the ancient Nazca people created shallow lines on the arid ground by moving aside the reddish iron oxide rocks to reveal the light gray ground beneath. The Lines are believed to have come into existence, with or without extraterrestrial assistance, between 500 B.C. and 500 A.D. They continue to be a phenomenon of wonder, mystery, and debate well into the twenty-first century.

The climate of the plateau is dry and windless, and the area of roughly 190 square miles is isolated. Thus, the drawings have remained stable for over two thousand years. The action of creating the lines by moving the small rocks is the easy part to explain. More problematic is how these ancient people mapped out massive designs with perfect lines, angles, and curves and, most mysteriously, *why*.

Some of my life's most splendid thrills have been the moments when I met for the first time a place, a structure, a work of art, or, as in the case of the gauchos, a people, that I had long studied in text, film, and photos and taught about in college classrooms. Yet, nothing I had ever seen in books, on TV, or in the grainy images in Von Däniken's book prepared me for what was beneath us on the Nazca Plain.

24

The Flyboys of the Nazca Plain

The Nazca Plain is crisscrossed with innumerable straight lines, intersecting and parallel, up to thirty miles long. The biomorphs (drawings of animals, plants, and humans) are between 440 and 1,200 feet in length. For the sake of comparison, 1,200 feet is close to the height of the Empire State Building, or about a quarter mile. It was the biomorphs for which I'd made Joyce eat dust with me during thirty hours of bouncing along unpaved roads to reach this site. I had clear mental pictures of the most well-known of these figures but actually seeing them from the window of a small plane was one of the great thrills of a lifetime.

Solón flew us over the Plain much longer than the thirty minutes our $15 fee had bought (now, it's about $120 including airport tax). In the dramatic splendor of our sky-high perspective, we saw the condor (440 feet long and almost equally as wide), and the hummingbird (320 by 216 feet), both in symmetry like an ancient hymn; the spider, 150 feet of magnificence in anatomical detail; the monkey (310 by 190 feet), with seven perfect concentric coils of tail; and dozens more including macaw, iguana, parrot, lizard, fish, pelican, killer whale, tree, flower, human figures, and the 935-foot heron. New drawings, including a cat, have been discovered in recent years.

After landing, we returned to the rundown building that was the airport lounge and sat around the table drinking a soda with Cholo

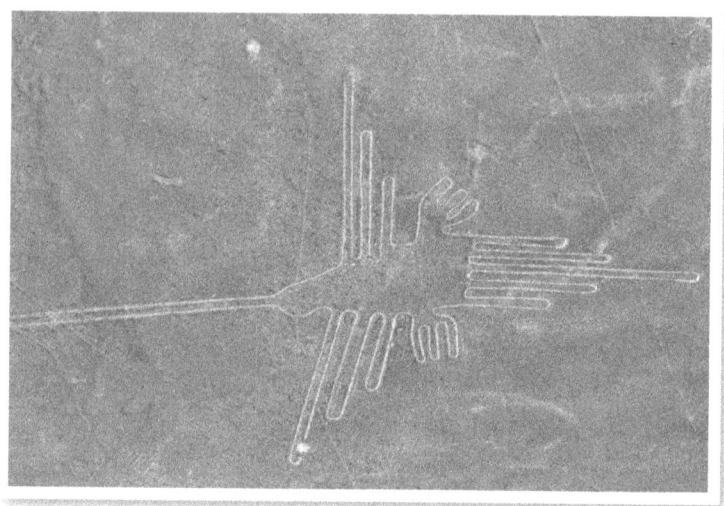

Hummingbird on the Plain of Nazca

and Solón and the other two pilots, Rolo and Jorge, all young guys in their twenties and early thirties. They spoke of how, theories of extraterrestrials aside, the lines and figures could have been made using rudimentary surveying techniques, a belief held by many archaeologists today, although a number maintain that some sort of manned flight would have been necessary to design and direct the creation of such huge, complex, and accurate drawings.

A mention of how the dry air and scant rainfall have preserved these drawings for over two millennia reminded them to show us their hidden surprise. Joyce and I followed them into a dim back room. They opened the bottom drawer of a filing cabinet, and I was horrified to be looking down into a dark brown, desiccated female face. They had found this naturally preserved mummy in the Nazca desert and decided to keep her at the airstrip as a bonus attraction for their passengers. After all these years, I still recoil at the recall of the crouched fold of the body and her tragic, withered face.

The American businessmen from Pennsylvania had finished their tour and flown back to Lima in their chartered Cessna 310. It was a slow afternoon, and Cholo offered to pass the rest of his shift by taking us up for another tour of the lines, this one *cortesía de la casa* — on the house. As the plane gained altitude, we began to dig deeper into the *why* of the Nazca Lines.

I had read about the German mathematician and archaeologist Maria Reiche and knew she had been living in Nazca and doing research to work out the meaning of the lines and figures since 1940 when she became the assistant to American historian Paul Kosok. The two postulated that the straight lines were part of a giant astronomical calendar pointing to the positions on the horizon where the sun rose or set on solstice days. Her mathematical calculations established the highly sophisticated precision of the animal, human, and plant figures on the plain. She theorized that the lines represented a huge astronomical calendar and that most of the figures depicted constellations. Just as we identify ours as animals and mythological beings (Scorpio: scorpion, Cetus: whale, Pisces: fish, Capricornus: goat; Phoenix, Orion, Hydra, etc.), Reiche believed that the ancient Nazca looked to the night sky and identified monkey, spider, hummingbird, condor, and so on.

Although her theory is not widely accepted today, Reiche's tireless lobbying for preservation of the site is the reason this immense cultural treasure is still intact. She convinced the government that the Peruvian Air Force had to make photographic surveys of the plain. She hired private security from her own funds to guard the perimeter of the site. She persuaded the government to restrict public access, and she sponsored the construction of a viewing tower that she hoped would keep visitors from trodding on the lines. Maria Reiche lived in Nazca until her death in 1998 and experienced the culmination of her life's work when the Nazca Lines were declared a UNESCO World Heritage Site in 1994.

Before we began our descent, Cholo suggested I take the controls for a few minutes and, although Joyce's wary eye from the back seat said, "Please don't," I did, and we survived my apprenticeship with Cholo guiding me on direction and altitude and taking back the controls to land us neatly on the dirt strip. He drove us back to town in his air-conditioned pickup, making it into a mini tour that included his small apartment, the archaeological museum, and a store where we could exchange traveler's checks for Peruvian *soles*, a pressing need since The Banco Nacional was *still* on strike after a month.

A couple of hours later, on the breezy veranda of the Nazca Tourist Hotel bar, a tropical oasis in the Peruvian desert, we met up again with Cholo, Rolo, and their friends Pucho and Carlos for pisco sours, group photos, and a lot of laughter as Cholo insisted on reading Joyce's palm, most probably just to have an excuse to hold her hand.

Cholo reading Joyce's palm

The best Chinese food I've ever eaten was in the *chifas* of Peru, and dinner that evening in the little Chinese restaurant called Chifa Chele was cheap but memorable as Joyce and I anticipated our next adventure. We had already bought our bus tickets to Lima for the next day, but when Cholo said he was going for business and offered to drive us, we only hesitated a second while recalling the day and a half of public transportation worse-than-purgatory that we had endured to get here. He hefted our bulging suitcases into the truck bed early the next morning and we hopped into the cab. Joyce nudged me to take the middle seat lest our driver be inspired to take his hands off the wheel to read her palm again. A few minutes after departure, Cholo pulled off the highway at Maria Reiche's viewing platform so we could make the climb to the top to see a drawing of hands and one of a bird. However, after having soared above the Nazca Lines, these earthbound views were only partial and could not compare with what we had experienced from the skies.

There are many more theories that attempt to explain how and why an ancient people created these endless straight lines and precise drawings that over two centuries later remain unsolved hieroglyphics stretching over nearly two hundred square miles of the Nazca Desert of southern Peru. They are yours to explore, dear reader, if you choose. For me, it was enough to have been there, to have experienced the magnificent drawings from the skies: undeciphered messages, huge and mysterious, the work of minds and hands of a bygone race. And who knows but, assisted or not by extraterrestrials, maybe they did it simply out of awe for the beauty and glory of the natural world. And because they found a way.

25

Lightening the Load in Lima

The Pan-American Highway from Nazca to Lima was desolate, but with Cholo at the wheel of his pickup, the miles flew by and the conversation was animated and bilingual. Joyce was making progress in Spanish, and Cholo knew enough English to fill in the blanks. As we drove past endless huge coastal sand dunes, Cholo commented that he made this drive frequently and the scenery shifted with each trip.

In the twenty-first century, some visitors do more than just admire the ever-changing mounds of sculpted sand—they surf them. Just nine miles east of Nazca is Cerro Blanco, known now as "The Everest of the Desert." At 6,824 feet, it's the highest dune in the world and boasts the boarder's fantasy of a two-thousand-foot slope. Huacachina in southwestern Peru has become another mecca for sandboarding, the latest in extreme sports that meets all the requirements of thrills and chills, speed and spills, and a great story to tell back at the bar. However, in our simpler era of the late twentieth century, it was just comfortably monotonous views of dune after dune towering in the shimmering heat, and our joy of *not* being on that slow, hot bus we just whizzed past, which wouldn't reach Lima until around midnight.

At 5:00 p.m., we said grateful goodbyes to Cholo on the steps of a suitable hotel in the upscale Miraflores district of Lima, knowing we would always hold warm memories of Nazca and the flyboys of the Plain. That evening in our hotel room, I wrote a long missive to Kevin about our adventures in Nazca, knowing he'd love reading about the flights over the Plain since he had piloted small planes since his teenage years. Our first date four years before was airborne to see Christo's fence, a work of art by Christo and Jeanne-Claude that used over two million square feet of white nylon fabric strung between steel poles for 25 miles through Sonoma and Marin counties of Northern California. It was a memorable sight that, like the lines of Nazca, could only be fully appreciated from a few thousand feet up.

Once in Lima and as promised, we visited David (of the Rupert/David Machu Picchu duo) at his apartment not far from our hotel. From that moment on, David became a defining presence of our stay in Lima because he was seriously smitten with Joyce. I was the third wheel and usually preferred to strike out on my own. It wasn't for lack of company that I felt lonely because I met locals and fellow travelers to share sightseeing and meals.

At the post office general delivery, I was ecstatic to get letters from my three best friends back home, Mónica, Christi, and Susan, but crestfallen that there was nothing from Kevin. The three months of roads traveled and another yet ahead sat heavy on my heart. If truth be told, to make matters worse, I was in a bout of bruised ego and feeling jealous of Joyce with a few unexpressed resentments added to the bitter mix. I knew I was being self-indulgent and petty, and that my envy over all the attention she got from the men we encountered was exaggerated by my dejection over Kevin's seeming indifference.

When I headed downtown by myself on day two, the afternoon took a dangerous turn. I was almost at the Plaza de Armas when tear gas started spewing, shopkeepers began slamming down metal doors, the Guardia Civil was running up and down side streets with machine guns, and the water tank trucks were tumbling protesters to the ground. I ran as fast as I could away from the action. The plaza remained closed by armed military for the remainder of our stay in Lima.

In a sunnier mood the following day, I wandered around Miraflores with Joyce until we came upon a pop-up market with the wares displayed on blankets laid out on the street. How odd that so much of what we glanced at was written in Chinese. I became enchanted with a display of exquisitely painted Chinese papercuts, and I knelt on the cobblestones to select a collection of the fragile pieces to take home. Little did we know that the riots in the plaza and the presence of Chinese books and crafts in the marketplace were connected dots and portents of Peru's civil war from 1980 to 2000 against The Shining Path (*El Sendero Luminoso*), a Maoist-inspired guerrilla movement.

The only cause of my homesickness was Kevin. I knew I was on the trip of a lifetime, having extraordinary experiences with unforgettable people. I even knew, despite my sometimes grumpiness, that I was showered with stardust to have Joyce as my traveling companion. But that boyfriend of mine was a constant in my mind, a mix of longing and desire, of uncertainty and preoccupation. I couldn't stand the isolation anymore. I needed to hear his voice.

After several hours of waiting in the Lima telephone office, the line was connected and we spoke for an exorbitant fifteen minutes about mail that never arrived, my return in August, and the effects of separation. He admitted this was harder on him than he had anticipated. He urged me to call him again, and in the warmth of this connection my insecurity and loneliness melted away. Of his solicitousness about a possible next phone call and when we would be together again, I wrote in my journal, "Ardent devotion, so sincere, painfully lacking in the past. We've turned a corner."

The afternoon Joyce and I spent at the hotel in Lima was consumed by rummaging through suitcases and totes to separate what we would keep for the last month of travel from what we would ship home. Since our arrival to Chile an age ago in April, our suitcases had grown from portly to obese. They were unwieldy beasts to begin with in those days before the invention of the rolling bag. Besides the accumulated gifts and souvenirs from Chile, Argentina, Uruguay, Brazil, and Paraguay, I hadn't been able to resist a five-by-seven-foot woven alpaca rug (an important player in a later chapter) and several other bulky textiles in the marketplaces of Bolivia. Those items, and the queen-sized crocheted bedspread Joyce had just bought the day before, were the final ten kilos that broke these travelers' backs.

It was going to cost much more than anticipated; we hadn't budgeted for this expense and didn't have the funds to cover it. We carried one credit card apiece, but since converting traveler's checks to local currency at the bank was still the standard, plastic cards were of very little use anywhere in South America in that pre-ATM era. We settled on sending the crate COD (Cash on Delivery) to Joyce's aunt and uncle in Sacramento, thus postponing the pain of payment until some future date. I was still aglow from my phone call with Kevin as I carefully tucked the woven straw airplane for my flyboy back home into the shipping box between the folds of the alpaca rug.

Only one evening left in Lima, yet there remained three unexpected initiations. For the first time, I tasted salty chips made from sweet potatoes, a Peruvian street food concept that would not reach the U.S. for another twenty years; I borrowed David's copy of *Cien años de soledad* (*One Hundred Years of Solitude*) and, for the first time, read lines by Gabriel García Márquez, the Colombian novelist and soon-to-be winner of the Nobel Prize for Literature in 1982; and I saw my first production of the musical *Man of La Mancha* (*El hombre de La Mancha*). Joyce enjoyed it even though she hadn't read *Don Quixote* and couldn't follow much of the dialogue, but recognized the tunes though sung in Spanish. I knew "The Impossible

Dream" by heart since the musical had hit Broadway in 1965, but it touched me to hear the eccentric knight sing in deep baritone with the conviction of unshakable idealism, "*El sueño imposible.*" Sitting in the small theater-in-the-round in Lima, I felt a wondrous wave of certainty that I was in the exact right place at the perfect moment. I felt inspired and full of possibility for the month of travel that lay ahead, and for the future beyond.

An oppressive layer of high fog called *la garúa* holds Lima hostage throughout the Peruvian winter from June to October. It is damp, chilly, relentless, and generally depressing. It was only July, and the Limeños had months to go before they would see the sun again. Not so for Joyce and me. En route to Ecuador, we had planned for a couple of days on the balmy northern coast of Peru. We were on our way to sunshine, sand, and surf by 6:30 a.m., suitcases blessedly lighter, and glad we hadn't shipped off our bikinis and beach towels in that cargo crate soon to be on a slow boat north to California.

26

The Surfing Horses of Huanchaco

An uneventful dozen hours of bus time took us north from Lima to Trujillo, a small city we didn't find particularly attractive, but we embraced it with enthusiasm as our gateway to the beach. It was July and still winter in the Southern Hemisphere, but Trujillo lived up to its reputation as "The City of Everlasting Spring." We reveled in its warm sunshine, but the real reason we were there was to get to Huanchaco. We threw on shorts and t-shirts over our swimsuits and caught the local bus for the five-mile ride to the coast.

In 1979, Huanchaco was just a small fishing village with the requisite church on the hill and three cafés. Now, it's a popular destination for surfers and tourists, and claims to be the birthplace of *ceviche*, chunks of raw fish marinated in lime and lemon juice. We would eat some of the best later in the day, but the first order was a long walk on the beach, talking to fishermen, and seeking out what back then was Huanchaco's greatest claim to fame, *los caballitos de totora*.

It wasn't long before we came upon a shirtless, burnished man straddling a huge wad of long reeds (*totora*: a species of giant bulrush sedge) and muscling the twine around and around to bind the stalks. He pointed up the beach where several men were angling their *caballitos* into the breaking surf and paddling out for the day's catch of crab. Do these sedge crafts resemble the "little horses" they are named for? Not at all, but the fishermen mount them and buck

Los caballitos de Huanchaco

the crest of breakers into deeper waters. The finished caballito is ten to twelve feet long, and its thin bow sweeps up out of the water Viking-style for stability afloat. Fishermen of the region have caught crab this way for over two thousand years.

This particular reed is found only in parts of South America and on Easter Island, a Polynesian territory of Chile, 2,290 miles off its coast. Even more famous than the caballitos of Huanchaco are the many ways totora is used on Lake Titicaca, the highest navigable lake in the world, on the border between Bolivia and Peru. Some of the Uros people still live on floating islands made by piling layer upon layer of this sedge. They use the reeds to fashion their homes, furniture, boats, and clothing, and a part of the reed is even a staple in their diet.

As the sun dipped toward the horizon, Joyce and I were on the patio of a café, enjoying superb ceviche and a cold beer, happy in each other's company and basking in the joy of a perfect day. We caught the bus back to Trujillo and were pleasantly surprised to learn there would be a performance of classical ballet that evening. We washed off salt and sand, made ourselves conservatively presentable, and headed for the theater. You shall soon find out why we ducked down side streets, trying not to attract attention along the way. Classical ballet it truly was, and in the audience, there were at least a hundred teenaged schoolboys who nearly drowned out the orchestra over everything they thought worthy of snickers.

On the way to the central market the next morning, it was the usual scene of dozens of men hanging out on street corners, seemingly their only purpose being to follow the urge to call out provocative phrases to every female passerby. Besides the local lovelies, we were often a target for *piropos* wherever we went as well, since there just weren't that many young American women making their way through South America in this era.

It's hard to understand this aspect of Latino culture (varying widely one country to another) from a twenty-first century, particularly American, point of view, but the *piropo* (pee-ROH-poh) is a sociolinguistic phenomenon deeply rooted in history, culture, and, yes, machismo. I had learned about piropos in graduate school from my fellow students and was fascinated by the creativity that the desire to impress a girl, and possibly advance admiration into courtship, could engender.

Piropos come in all sizes and colors. Some are so vulgar as to singe the ears, though I suspect given today's acceptance of all manner of sexual bluntness, those piropos don't have the "firepower" they once packed. The word derives from the Greek *pyros* meaning "fire," and *ops*, "face": "fire in the face." Hmmm, would that be the passion of the man who launches it, or the deep blush of the woman who receives it but, by cultural commandment, pretends not to notice?

In the central market, we bought picnic supplies for another perfect beach day in Huanchaco with some travelers we'd met the day before: four bananas, two chirimoyas (exotic fruit, looks like a hand grenade, may be aphrodisiac), four tangerines, a huge avocado called *palta* in these parts, four slices of bread, a package of cheese, a lime, and some salt—all for the equivalent of one dollar. Returning to our hotel from the market, I thought more about piropos and how we should react.

Many of the piropos we heard in Trujillo were banal and totally lacking in originality or individuality. The most common and annoying call was *¡Tst-tst!*, the sound a person might make to rudely call a waiter's attention in a café. Another one-size-fits-all, *¡Preciosa!*, did not merit a blink either. But declaring a true piropo lives up to its synonym: *echar una flor*. If the man "tosses a flower," he has said something complimentary, captivating, and perhaps even meaningful to the woman he wants to impress. His words come from piropo tradition or straight from his imagination but, either way, they carry a measure of poetic creativity that propels the phrase to his intended.

My all-time favorite piropo for pure ingenuity and adorable charm applies to a situation where boy spies girl hooked to the arm of and under the watchful eye of her mother, and he says to the mamá: "*Vaya con Dios, señora . . . ¡y su hija conmigo!*" — May you go with God, ma'am [a blessing] . . . and your daughter with me! When the besotted young man sees a vision dressed in blue, he might exclaim, "*¡Con tan poco azul, tanto cielo!*" — With so little blue, so much sky! The most *escandaloso* piropo my friends taught me might seem tame by modern sensibilities, but it crosses the line with its clear sexual reference: His attention glued to a great pair of legs, he says, — "*¡Qué rieles! ¿Cómo será la estación?*" — What rails! I wonder what the station is like?

The custom of "tossing a flower" was not originally intended to devalue, demean, or harass a woman. However, times have changed, and now just bringing up the topic of piropos means skating on thin ice. Our word "catcalls" is perhaps even too gentle a term for the sexual harassment aimed at women on streets worldwide. However, from a historical perspective, the piropo at least deserves notice, if not appreciation, as a creative solution to "how to get her to notice me noticing her" in a bygone era of stifling social norms.

Will the piropo survive in modern times, and should it? Another perfect day at the beach, then the walk from the bus stop back to the hotel, punctuated by endless iterations of ¡*Tst-tst!* and ¡*Preciosa!* gave me more time to think this over.

27

Piropos: Sweet, Spicy, and Banned

As a literary and social tradition, *piropos* are the echo of an earlier age of courtship when boy couldn't just meet girl, have a chat, and suggest a date for Friday night. There were layers of social obstacles with which to contend, including parents, protective brothers, maiden aunts, chaperones, and often, an arranged marriage already etched into the stony imagination of the older generation. What was a poor fellow to do? Ah-ha! The imagination kicks in and he composes an enticing *piropo*, then waits where he hopes she might pass—the church door on Sunday is always a good bet—so he can toss his verbal "flower," make his intentions known, and hope for a blushing glance in his direction.

Here is a selection of classics that may cause a roll of the eyes, but there is a flavor of generosity, creativity, and even sweetness about them:

¡Quien fuera bizco para verte dos veces!
("Oh, to be cross-eyed and see you twice!")
¿Qué hace una estrella volando tan bajito?
("What is a star doing flying so low?")
¿Qué estará sucediendo en el cielo que los ángeles se están cayendo?
("What could be happening in heaven for angels to be falling to earth?")

¡Ahora resulta que las estatuas caminan!
("Now it turns out that statues can walk!")
¡Tú eres mi catedral; las demás son capillitas!
("You are my cathedral; the rest are little chapels!")
¿De qué juguetería te escapaste, muñeca?
("Which toy store did you escape from, doll?")
Por un besito, ni dos, ¡a nadie castiga Dios! (Notice the rhyme.)
("For a little kiss or two, God won't punish anyone!")
¡No cierres los ojos porque quedo a oscuras!
("Don't close your eyes because I'll be left in the dark!")
¡Dime cómo te llamas, y te pongo en mi lista de deseos!
("Tell me your name, and I'll put you on my wish list!")

If Joyce and I had heard anything that charming on the streets of Trujillo, La Paz, or Buenos Aires, we might have broken the code of indifference and at least cracked a smile. The piropos we heard were more in the unimaginative vein of "Hey, baby!" You can tell by my stories that we befriended locals everywhere we traveled, but not the ones who tried to get our attention with harassment.

That said, creative suggestiveness is more interesting than uninspired banality—at least in print. (The reality on the street can be harsh and threatening. More on that in a moment.)

Here are a few piropos on the wilder side:

¡Prefiero los días de viento para faldas como ésa!
("I prefer windy days for skirts like that one!")
¡Quisiera ser chocolate para derretirme en tu boca!
("I wish I were chocolate so I could melt in your mouth!")
¡Qué curvas, y yo sin frenos!
("What curves, and I without brakes!")
¡Quien fuera pulmón para vivir en tu pecho!
("Oh, to be a lung and live inside your chest!")

¡Quien fuera músico para tocar semejante guitarra!
("Oh, to be a musician and finger such a guitar!")
Si te falta la respiración, ¡yo tengo un curso en primeros auxilios!
("If you feel breathless, I'm trained in first aid!")
¡Quisiera ser yo el sol para poder calentarte todo el día!
("I would like to be the sun to heat you up all day long!")

Yes, times have changed and there's nothing innocent about piropos anymore. A catcall on the street is recognized as demeaning and threatening to women, and an act of aggression. A 2016 law in Argentina outlawed piropos as constituting sexual harassment, a misdemeanor punishable by a fine of up to 1,000 pesos (about $120) or five days in jail. Peru, Chile, Costa Rica, Nicaragua, and other Latin American countries have already passed or are working on legislation to ban piropos. Of course, this is an international issue and it's not only Latin American countries that are seeking to respond. Many U.S. states and cities have laws against verbal harassment, but they are hard to enforce, and even the line between what constitutes an infringement is wavy.

Just when I'd concluded that the true "flower" of the piropo had been choked out by weeds of vulgarity and downright harassment, I came across the two catchy phrases that follow. We can't know if anyone from the digital age would actually utter such words, but we can be sure that *someone* out there is injecting new creativity into a very old tradition.

Behold, the modern piropo:

Seguro que te apellidas Google, bonita, ¡porque tienes todo lo que estaba buscando!
("Your last name must be Google, cutie, because you have everything I've been looking for!")

Si tus labios fueran un puerto USB, ¡me mantendría conectado todo el tiempo!
("If your lips were a USB port, I'd stay connected all the time!")

Was the piropo only launched from the rage of hormones toward the bloom of youth? In fact, there are many lovely piropos that praise and admire the qualities of women "of a certain age":

¡Las mujeres son como el vino, y tú eres la gran reserva!
("Women are like wine, and you are the 'grand reserve'!")
¡Cada año que tienes es un punto más de esplendor!
("Each year you have is yet another stitch of splendor!")
¡El mejor adorno para tu preciosa cara son las canas que la enmarcan!
("The best adornment for your precious face is the gray hair that frames it.")

Okay, so they seem more like piropos that would be exclaimed at one's retirement dinner or eightieth birthday party, but they *are* in the canon, and at the time of this writing, I would not be offended to hear one of those "flowers" tossed across my aging path.

But for now, it's still 1979, and I've still got that "bloom of youth." So, ¡adiós, Perú—we are headed for Ecuador, out to the Galápagos Islands, and back for a surprise romantic encounter.

28

The Difficult Door to Ecuador

Thus far, we had made seven border crossings from one South American country to another, and experience had taught us that these take time, patience, and a bizarre sense of humor with no expectation for logic to prevail. The crossing from Peru into Ecuador took the record for length of time, frazzled nerves, and downright weirdness. After the overnight bus from Trujillo to the border, it took six hours to actually complete the crossing into Ecuador.

As our passports were checked at the first station, I kept a wary eye on one of the guards sprawled in an office chair toying with his loaded pistol. Two officials went through everyone's hand luggage, then we reboarded and the bus was allowed to proceed a few feet after which nothing happened for two hours. The baffling wait ended with another passport check and full baggage customs. The baggage reloaded, we all cheered as the driver fired up the engine and the bus got underway. First gear into second, second gear into third, we settled into our seats, finally making progress on Ecuadorian soil.

Suddenly, more border police pulled the bus over, and we were ordered to exit with only passport in hand and wait at the side of the road. They called this a passport check, but we were convinced it was a ploy to get us off the bus so they could go through our belongings again, looking for contraband, drugs, bugs, or . . . ? We boarded again and nervously checked our wallets, happy to still be in possession of our *sucres*, but wisely stuffing this local currency into our pockets for the rest of the trip.

The next "leg" was only slightly longer. About a half mile down the road, we were stopped by yet another group of border officials, all armed with machine guns. They ordered us off and then combed through the bus, taking every book in sight. For the second time during this continental odyssey, I was in a panic at the prospect of losing my indispensable *South American Handbook*. After a long, hand-wringing wait, they returned everyone's books and hustled us back on board, having just fumigated the bus with something that smelled like chlorine, perhaps to ensure no Peruvian *bichos* had hitchhiked their way into Ecuador. I wondered if they checked between all the pages of our books for clandestinely traveling bugs as well.

Since then, I have been back to Ecuador five times, but returning to Quito in the twenty-first century, I didn't recognize anything in the old historic downtown of this nosebleed-high capital city.[3] That was a good thing because in 1979, it was quite run down with crumbly structures and unlit, claustrophobic streets. The urban renewal project began in 2002 with an injection of new businesses, marketplaces, hotels, and dwellings. The refurbishing of churches and government buildings and superb illumination showing off their tasteful new pastel colors made everything safer, more attractive, and more accessible, while maintaining the flavor and charm of "old" Quito.

During delightful days in Quito, we listened to Andean folk music played on pan pipes (*zampoña*) and flute (*quena*), ate Chinese food in the *chifas* because, as in Peru, they served the best cheap food in

---

3. Speaking of nosebleeds, it's worth noting that the four highest capital cities in the world are in South America: La Paz, Bolivia at 11,942 feet (the seat of the legislative and executive branches of the government); Quito, Ecuador at 9,350 feet; Sucre, Bolivia at 9,220 feet (the seat of the judicial branch of government); and Bogotá, Colombia at 8,612 feet.

town, and befriended a dozen American Peace Corps volunteers because the city was crawling with them. This made for interesting nightlife while many of our daylight hours were spent visiting the nearby indigenous market villages of Saquisilí and Otavalo.

In Saquisilí we took an early-morning stroll through the cemetery to pass the time before the market got underway and to thaw out from the pre-dawn chill of the bus ride. A troop of gravediggers materialized from the mist, hard at work excavating the final resting place for a recently deceased local whose cadaver and funeral entourage would soon arrive.

They were a cheerful, motley band with picks and shovels, patched pants, and only a few remaining teeth to flash in wide smiles. I said hello and they welcomed the interruption to take a break from digging. One of the men pulled a bottle of *aguardiente* out of his back pocket, literally "fire water": *agua* (water), *ardiente* (burning). With a gapey grin and crinkled eyes, he extended a brimming plastic shot cup in our direction, some of the clear liquid sloshing over the top. Joyce wanted none of this interaction with the ragtag group and sidled over to the fence. I accepted the grimy little cup and sipped, hoping the fire water would kill the bacteria on the cup itself and any that might survive as far as my gut.

We had a convivial chat, accompanied by a few more shots of *aguardiente* passed around and toasts to health, family, and happy life. Sensing that the new resident of this hole they were employed to dig was soon approaching, we began our goodbyes. I took a photo of the lot of them and jotted down an address, promising to send it when I got back to California and had my pictures developed. To this day, it is a regret that burns. I never did. It was probably the only photograph ever taken of any of them.

After the market visit, we boarded a local bus to return to Quito. The guidebook said the views of volcanoes would be magnificent

The gravediggers of Saquisilí

in and around the city, but the sky was heavily overcast with not a peak in sight. Suddenly, Joyce pointed to a perfect volcano on a far, far horizon, briefly illuminated by a blaze of sun from behind the clouds that burned the image into my memory forever.

Joyce and I had deliberated mightily in choosing the one big excursion we could afford to take. Would we fly west to the Galápagos Islands, or travel east into the Amazon rainforest? Back in California, we had debated as to which natural wonder would likely be the first ruined by human "progress." Ultimately, we opted to visit the Galápagos, hoping the jungle would survive until a future trip.

Since that first flight into the Pacific off the coast of Ecuador, I have been to the Islands four more times: three with study/travel groups from my college, and one with three teenaged nephews. Lucky me that on all four of those subsequent Ecuador trips, we also spent several days deep in the jungles of Amazonia in what is called the *Oriente* of Ecuador. What a gift that the experience of both marvelous wonders came to me again not just once, but multiple times. However, the first time in Galápagos was a true rough-and-ready adventure and one that, like our experience of Machu Picchu, could never be duplicated in modern times.

29

The Galápagos: A Past Perfect Paradise, Part I

We had traveled from Quito to the coastal city of Guayaquil because it had the only airport with flights to the Galápagos Islands. Stretching our purse strings, Joyce and I scoured the city's tour agencies for an affordable five-day boat excursion and wondered, *Could we spring for this and still have the funds to complete our continental trajectory through Colombia and ultimately to Mónica's in the Dominican Republic?* We compared, we debated, and we purchased the cheapest excursion we could find from Antonio at Budget Tours in a shabby downtown storefront.

Back then, there was one flight per week to the Galápagos; now there are several a day into two island airports from both Guayaquil and Quito. Tourism to the Galápagos has been on a galloping increase since the '70s with over 300,000 visitors per year today paying an entrance fee of $200 per person. In 1979 there was no fee, and we were two of only about ten thousand tourists to the Islands. Operators and guides didn't have to be licensed, and there were no injunctions about much of anything except "Don't stray from the paths and don't touch the wildlife." During our five days at sea, we visited seven islands but seldom saw more than two other boats. The one I lusted after was a sleek red sloop that leapfrogged us from one mooring to the next. (I was an avid ocean sailor in those days and had a passion for big boats and rough seas.) Today there are hundreds of licensed tour craft and a big port in the bustling little city of Puerto Ayora, population 13,000, on Santa Cruz Island.

On our last evening at the *pensión* in Guayaquil before our morning flight to the Islands, Joyce and I were feeling excited, restless, and celebratory, so we set our sights on an upscale establishment for dinner in what was otherwise a dirty and oppressively humid city. The meal at the Hotel Continental was an extravagance at $5 apiece for three courses including wine. Two good-looking men at the adjoining table were speaking German and they gallantly introduced themselves when they realized we were Americans. (We thought we were being coy by speaking Spanish.)

We had a friendly visit over an hour of dessert and coffee. Heinrich was Swiss, worked for a multinational corporation, and lived in a gated community in Guayaquil. Franz, also Swiss and employed by the same company, was on a business trip to Ecuador and staying at Heinrich's estate. We described the trajectory of our travels during the past three months and our plan to fly to Galápagos the next day, then we said our goodbyes and exchanged well-wishes for whatever life might bring. When Franz casually popped in to kiss Joyce's hand at breakfast the next morning in the *pensión*, I suspected paths would cross again.

As we started our flight over 780 miles of ocean in a big, noisy prop plane, we settled into the seats with light hearts and huge sighs of relief because Antonio had been late showing up at the airport with our tickets. At 9:15 the agent announced he would sell our seats to stand-by passengers if Antonio didn't show by 9:30. I was frantic and yelling into the pay phone to Budget Tours, "Antonio, *¿dónde está usted*? We need you here *now*!" Antonio charged in with tickets in hand at the last minute, and three hours later we made a bumpy landing at the airstrip in Baltra, formerly a U.S. Army Air Force Base during World War II.

I couldn't wait to set foot on the volcanic earth. The Galápagos Islands were formed by some of the most active oceanic volcanoes in the world and, at about five million years old, they are relatively young compared to most of our planet's other islands. The archipelago is one of the most richly biodiverse places on earth, as we were soon to experience through all five of our senses.

When we finally arrived at the dock from the airport by bus and ferry—it wouldn't have been a proper South American bus ride if there hadn't been an unexplained two-hour delay—I registered heat, blinding sun, lava rock surroundings, barren ground dotted with cactus, the fishy smell of the day's catch, and fat yellow iguanas in motionless reception of this small batch of humans invading their paradise. Two giant pelicans danced a raucous welcome on the dock, but once they flew off there was absolute quiet. The turquoise water was so invitingly clear! Little did we know it would be our only "bath" for the next five days.

In 2012, I took my three teenaged nephews to experience the wonders of Ecuador and the Galápagos Islands. We were on a lovely island cruiser with twelve cabins, gourmet meals, wetsuits and snorkel gear, deck chairs, and en suite bathrooms with hot showers. I felt so pampered, I didn't even mind having to share a cabin with fifteen-year-old Jonathan. I reminisced to the boys about my economy cruise thirty-three years earlier . . .

We were ten passengers on a 25-foot boat named "*Gavi*", short for *gaviota* (seagull). Along with Joyce and me, there was Tim from New York, a threesome from Switzerland, an Uruguayan couple with a little boy, and a French girl, Isabel, whom we adopted as our third "musketeer." The crew consisted of Guillermo, guide and *capitán*, and his *asistente*, Jorge. Each of us had a short, narrow wooden bunk

Joyce and Isabel in the Galápagos

with something padded that might be called a mattress, a lumpy pillow, and light bedding. For the needs of the twelve of us, there was one tiny head with a toilet and wash basin. No shower. My first night onboard was restless. I awakened repeatedly to the sound of one or more rats gnawing noisily behind the thin wood separating my head from the innards of the boat. Well, if this was to be the soundtrack of my Galápagos nights aboard the *Gavi*, I had best start practicing acceptance.

Guillermo and Jorge always trolled a fishing line off the back of the boat. Whatever they caught made for wonderfully fresh lunches and dinners supplemented by squash, beans, pasta, rice, or potatoes. For breakfast, there was fruit, eggs, bread, cheese, and coffee. Bottled water wasn't plentiful, but Coca-Cola was ubiquitous and always the preferred drink in South America over any other form of non-alcoholic hydration. Of course, the rum flowed freely for this was, after all, life on the high seas.

From my Galápagos experience with nephews in 2012 as well as three other trips I led for Spanish-learning adults from 2007 to 2009, I can report that the Islands are still a paradise, though less than "perfect." In addition to ever-burgeoning numbers of tourists, there are more regulations as well as ecological problems with overpopulation, illegal encroachment onto national park lands, and the ravages of non-native animals (pigs, goats, chicken, cats, dogs, and rats) and invasive plants.

Since 1998, contenders for the highly coveted jobs as Galápagos tour guides must be permanent residents of the Islands and pass an intensive education and training program to obtain the license that then must be renewed every two years. Twenty years before the Ecuadorian government established legal measures for the protection of the Galápagos, it seems all one needed to run an operation like Guillermo's was to have a boat, and if *Gavi* was an indication of standards, *any* boat would do. However, there were no complaints from Joyce and me. This was a dream come true, and the absence of a shower, snorkels, or a refrigerator, plus the presence of rats in the hold, and the strange behavior of first-and-only-mate Jorge, were minor and often humorous inconveniences as we toured the incomparable natural wonders of the Galápagos.

30

The Galápagos: A Past Perfect Paradise, Part II

The first indication that our crewman Jorge was a shady character came on the second night of our Galápagos boat trip when Joyce, Isabel, and I hopped into the dinghy with Capitán Guillermo and Jorge to visit the crew and passengers of a nearby cruiser. As Jorge imbibed rum, he became ever more insistent in his attempts to "comfort" Isabel, who was slightly seasick but not interested in his help. The next day, hungover, hangdog, and hell-bent on gaining her favor, he took every opportunity to bring her sodas and little gifts, bowing and scraping over his behavior the night before.

Joyce and one of the Swiss girls—trying to ignore Jorge

Each of our days was spent ashore exploring a different island and swimming in endless expanses of crystalline waters. On Santa Cruz, we visited the giant Galápagos tortoises the islands are named after at the Charles Darwin Center in Puerto Ayora. Nature documentaries do not prepare one for the impact of a direct experience with these massive reptiles, and that's why they will get a chapter all to themselves. When I witnessed a copulation, the male rearing high into the air atop the female while moaning and bellowing, and on another occasion, a battle between two males, I stopped describing these majestic creatures with adjectives such as "slow" and "passive."

Tortoises mating—anything but "slow" and "passive"

After our introduction to this iconic animal of the islands, we focused our fascination on sea lions, iguanas, flamingos, penguins, and the blue-footed boobies with their big fluffy chicks. This bird's webbed feet are a stunning bright blue, especially during mating season when the male struts to and fro raising those flashy blues to beak level at the female, hoping she will give him the nod to start nest-building. They ignored our presence as we walked the marked paths, often so close we could have reached out and touched them.

Of course, we didn't because this was forbidden by park regulations even then, and because the proximity of humans *not* making attempts at physical contact contributes to why most of the Galápagos fauna are unafraid of humans into the twenty-first century. Even sea lions lolled and played near us on the beaches, unfazed by our company. Nevertheless, we stepped carefully, for a bull could become aggressive in defense of his territory and his harem. The only diving equipment onboard the *Gavi* was a single face mask. We passengers took turns using it, and between gulps of air, I spotted spiny urchins and starfish, rays, marine turtles, and a Galápagos reef shark grazing the bottom for small fish and octopi.

While Guillermo was cleaning the first big fish caught on the trolling line, we threw pieces of skin to the enormous frigate birds hovering over the boat with their signature bright red inflated chest globes, and to the hungry pelicans floating at the stern. On day three, we motored to a spot frequented by the Galápagos penguins, the only native penguin species north of the equator, and one of the smallest in the world. I fell in love with these adorable little doll-like creatures. There were several of them shoulder-to-shoulder on a small dock gazing out to sea, perhaps bewildered by how their forebears had arrived at this rocky place and managed to adapt to the equatorial climate so far from their long-lost relatives in frigid Antarctica.

That evening, Guillermo and two captains from nearby boats took the dinghy to go *langostiando* — diving for lobsters. Along with trolling fishing lines from the back of the boat, this is now heavily regulated by Ecuadorean law, and tour boat operators can lose their license over illegal fishing. A chill ran down my spine to think of them diving in black waters in the dark of night, and time seemed to crawl as we passengers nervously listened for the sound of the little outboard motor returning to the *Gavi*. Yes, we wanted a moonlight lobster dinner, but we wanted our captain back even more. Jorge could surely navigate back to port, but he had become increasingly annoying, combative, and unpredictable. He kept up attempts to woo Isabel throughout the days, and she continued evasive maneuvers, including diving into the ocean for impromptu swims because on this small cabin cruiser there was no place to hide. When Guillermo wasn't there to keep Jorge in line, Joyce and I played bodyguards and ran interference for our friend.

As soon as the three captains disappeared into the inky waters, Jorge had the rum bottle in hand and launched into a string of bawdy songs and jokes punctuated by outbursts of anger at Guillermo, "*un capitán abusivo*," in the hope we would sympathize with him. At last, we spotted the dinghy's little light bobbing in the distance, and the lobster feasts for that night's dinner and the next day's lunch were worth the worry. We applauded our capitán's bravery and culinary skills but said nothing to him about Jorge.

When we arrived back in Puerto Ayora, Guillermo went ashore for supplies, and we were sorry to see him go because we knew what would happen next. Jorge started another rant against his employer, taking the show even farther this time, asking us passengers to side with him. He was taking this act too far, and when everyone had gone below to pack, I initiated a friendly chat and suggested that when he criticized the captain behind his back, it only served to make us uncomfortable and *less* sympathetic toward him. He started to sulk, but his anger didn't erupt until I said, "And please wash your hands after repairing the toilet and before preparing the meal." After dinner and more of his complaints to the group, he apologized to me profusely, but not sincerely, and begged me not to write a negative report on him. After fawning over the Uruguayan couple, he told their little boy to make sure *papá* gave him a big tip.

Guillermo returned early the next morning with oranges, cheese, sodas, matches, and a new second mate for the Gavi's next boatload of tourists. When we finished our final Galápagos outing to Caleta Tortuga for a closeup of marine turtles, Jorge was recklessly warning the new crewman about the "devil" in Guillermo, of which I'd yet to see a sign. At the Baltra Ferry for the bus trip to the airport, the Uruguayan couple told our capitán they wanted part of their money back because one of them had been obliged to share the tiny bunk with their five-year-old son.

Joyce, Isabel, and I were salty, sticky, and desperately in need of a head-to-toe scrubbing, but despite the grime we were aglow with our Galápagos experience. We'd gotten more than our meager money's worth in natural beauty, adventure, wonder, drama, rum 'n' coke, and fresh fish. I was not feeling jolly about the uninvited travelers in my gut (the first and only in this continental odyssey) that were causing me some intestinal problems, but, on the whole, we were awed, happy, and sunburned. Life was good. We didn't know it yet, but it was about to take off on an unanticipated new course as soon as our prop plane landed in Guayaquil.

I will tell all . . . but first, those iconic tortoises and how Lonesome George became their most famous ambassador in the world.

31

The Legacy of Lonesome George

Before we leave the Galápagos and return to Guayaquil, those massive reptiles for which the Islands are named deserve a chapter of their own. Joyce and I visited the Charles Darwin Research Center where Galápagos tortoises are bred and reared, and it was there that I met Lonesome George for the first time. He was in his mid-sixties and still in his prime, but despite dedicated attempts at matchmaking during his forty years at the Center, he remained "lonesome." George had been transported from Pinta Island of the Galápagos archipelago in 1972 because he was the only remaining tortoise on the island and was believed to be the last of his species.

Over his years of coddled and celebrated captivity, scientists arranged mating opportunities with females of his closest genetic match. I visited George again in 2007, 2008, and 2009 with my study/travel groups, always hoping for news of the birth of a little Georgie or Georgina. Alas, his would-be consorts did produce offspring with males of their own species, but George died in 2012 without an heir, and his subspecies was declared extinct.

Lonesome George's death was an international shock, for at an estimated age of one hundred years, he was still fairly young and, although overweight, was assessed by scientists to be in good health. In 2006, "Harriet" died from heart failure at age 176 in the Australia Zoo which was owned by "Crocodile Hunter" Steve Irwin and his wife, Terri. It is claimed that Harriet was one of three tortoises taken to Britain by Charles Darwin when she was about five years old and the size of a dinner plate. One of the oldest tortoises on record was "Tu'i Malila" from Madagascar, captured by Captain James Cook and gifted to the royal family of Tonga in the 1770s. She died in 1965 at the venerable age of 189. When "Adwaita" died in India in 2006, he had outlived so many caretakers that his age could only be estimated at between 150 and 250 years. Imagine having a pet in the back yard that was born around the time of the American Revolution!

In 1882, "Jonathan" was transported from his birthplace in the Seychelles to St. Helena, a British territory in the South Atlantic Ocean. Records confirm that he was fully mature at that time, which meant he was at least fifty years old. His birthdate has been set at no later than 1832, three years before Charles Darwin's historic voyage, and the year Andrew Jackson, the seventh U.S. president, was re-elected. In 2025, Jonathan's age is estimated at 192 years. He is the oldest living terrestrial vertebrate on earth, has lived through forty U.S. presidents, and is a celebrity of wide renown with the St. Helena five-pence coin sporting his image. Although he is blind from cataracts and has lost his sense of smell, caretakers report that his libido is still intact for he tries to mate with the male and female giant tortoises he lives with. His hearing is still sharp, and he has a big appetite for a wide range of fruits and vegetables.

Another "rock star" on the stage of giant tortoises is Diego, the now-legendary lover, originally from Española Island, Galápagos where he may have been taken in the 1930s, and formerly of the San Diego Zoo. Diego is now around 150 years of age and has a sex drive credited with helping save his species. According to reports from the Galápagos Conservancy, Española had only twelve females and two males left when Diego was introduced into the Galápagos National Park Restoration Breeding Program. After much highly productive amorous activity at the park, Diego was given a retirement pass (with a royal reptilian handshake) from the program when the subspecies count reached two thousand from the original fourteen. Paternity tests trace 40 percent of those progenerations back to Diego.

Now, he has been repatriated to his birthplace on Española Island, reunited with his consorts and several generations of offspring. Can Diego survive in the wild after nearly a century of fruity mocktails and room service? Fitted with a GPS, Diego is monitored six times a day by the Galápagos Conservancy staff, who constantly check on his whereabouts and activities. The GC reports that, over the past two years, he has become quite acclimated to his wild homeland while establishing his territory in an ever-wider arc. He may be retired from the official breeding program, but it appears Diego is still enthusiastically ensuring the continuation of his genetic line.

When Charles Darwin visited the Islands in 1835, there were fifteen subspecies of giant tortoises spread over twenty-one large and small Galápagos Islands. Today there remain ten, both a great loss and an amazing victory because their path to extinction seemed inevitable until rescue and protection efforts began in 1959 with the establishment of the Galápagos National Park and the Charles Darwin Foundation. Tortoises are by far the record holders for terrestrial vertebrate longevity, and the Galápagos varieties are the largest in the world. While not quite the size of my '63 Volkswagen Bug, some individuals measure over five feet in length and can weigh 550 pounds.

The fact that tortoises can live for up to a year without food or water is a grand advantage in the game of survival. However, it brought them to the brink of extinction because of their primary enemy—man. In the eighteenth and nineteenth centuries, buccaneers and whalers routed their voyages through the Galápagos Islands to capture live tortoises, which they stacked to the rafters in the holds of ships as a source of fresh meat for the duration of the voyage. Tortoises were also hunted for their oil, which was used as lamp fuel. The Galápagos Conservancy, an organization dedicated to the long-term preservation of the Islands, estimates that between 100,000 and 200,000 tortoises were sacrificed to human needs during those two centuries.

Since that time, an even more lethal threat is animals introduced by man, including goats, pigs, donkeys, rats, dogs, and cats. Animals introduced to the Islands have taken a tremendous toll on the tortoise populations. The females dig nest holes, lay their eggs, cover them, and leave. The eggs hatch in four to eight months, and baby tortoises in the wild are defenseless, thus easy prey for feral animals on the prowl for a meal, especially rats, pigs, dogs, cats, and invasive ants. Scientists collect eggs from areas on the islands where they are most vulnerable and hatch the baby tortoises in captivity until they are mature enough to fend for themselves.

In the wild, the tortoises are in competition for food and habitat with donkeys, pigs, goats, and other large animals that destroy the vegetation essential to the diet of these giant reptiles. Non-native species of plants, especially quinine and blackberry, are dense and prolific, causing the loss of natural food sources and territory. It is easy to imagine how much habitat is lost to rampant dense thickets of blackberry growing up to thirteen feet tall.

On Pinta Island, Lonesome George's birthplace, his species was believed to be extinct by the early twentieth century. On its website, the Galápagos Conservancy reports that in 1959, a group of fishermen released three goats on Pinta Island to ensure a new source of fresh meat on their long voyages at sea. By 1970 when George was first identified, the goat population had grown from three to 10,000, had fully occupied the island, and had noshed through all the vegetation available, including the cacti that were the staple of the tortoise diet. It is a miracle and a mystery that George survived.

Even though his direct lineage has ended, his legacy lives on as a symbol of species preservation worldwide. Inscribed on the wall outside of his enclosure at the Charles Darwin Research Center are these words: "Whatever happens to this single animal, let him always remind us that the fate of all living things on Earth is in human hands."

32

Swept Away

Joyce, Isabel, and I schlumped out of the plane, grubby and sticky from days of "bathing" in ocean water. Walking across the tarmac, we agreed there was nothing more we wanted from this humid, sprawling city than to be reunited with our luggage, get deep-cleaned in a hot shower, and have a tranquil night of sleep in anything wider than a two-foot bunk. We stepped inside the one-room terminal and were surprised to see a familiar face. Heinrich was waiting with cold sodas in an ice chest and an air-conditioned car to whisk us to his estate in a gated community of Guayaquil. It was, in a word, unreal!

After a quick pass by our hotel to pick up the luggage we had left in storage, he led us through a side entrance to our own private wing to get cleaned up and then join a big party of his international friends just going into full swing. I don't remember details about the individual guests, but I recall they were an eclectic group of Ecuadorean nationals and European ex-patriots steeped in adventure, international business, and money, with a dash of glitz.

After a glorious hour of taking turns at hot water, soap, and shampoo, we made our entrance onto the scene. Franz was beside himself to see the beautiful Joyce again. And Heinrich? Well, although we girls had resolved among ourselves to stay only one night and move on in the morning, it was only Isabel who did so. One night turned into two, and then to four as we went to the beach, ate ceviche, told adventure stories over gin and tonics, watched nature films Heinrich had produced, and disapprovingly admired the ocelot and parrots he kept caged in the yard.

We basked in the luxury of this unexpected soft landing into comfort, style, and the coddled confidence of not having to attend to basic daily demands for shelter, food, and transportation. The other thing I was basking in was Heinrich's attentive presence and fascinating conversation. He was a tall, handsome man of daring pursuits, and the photos lining the walls were a testament to his appetite for risk and adventure. Franz was clearly infatuated with Joyce, and she too was lapping up the attention and the luxurious lifestyle this hiatus offered.

By the time Heinrich took Joyce and me to the bus bound for Colombia, I was stary-eyed and smitten but didn't accept his invitation to stay longer. I was committed to finishing the trip with Joyce, committed to remaining faithful to the boyfriend back home, and committed to not getting involved with a married man. They had separated several months before, and his wife had moved back to Europe to "sort things out."

After these idyllic four days, the scene at the bus station was a chaotic jolt back to the reality of the road: tickets oversold, two people had taken our reserved seats, and there was no room for our luggage. We wrestled and squeezed bodies and suitcases until we got everything aboard this latest iteration of life in a sardine can. I commandeered the window and reached out to take Heinrich's hand. It was an awkward and unsatisfying farewell: "Thank you so much—for everything," with much left unsaid. Over the next months, we exchanged a few letters. I never found out what happened with his marriage.

The trip from Ecuador to Colombia was two days of self-doubt and daydreams, ending with the reality of being deposited in downtown Bogotá, at that time the city reputed to be the most dangerous in

South America. Nearly every traveler we talked to had been the victim or the witness of *delincuencia* (street crime) in Colombia, and we two seasoned travelers were determined to navigate without fear, but with attention and smart strategy. After all, we'd been through nine countries and had even plied the beaches and byways of Rio de Janeiro, another high-alert city, with my very rudimentary Portuguese and without a contrary incident.

That said, the fact that I put us on the wrong bus the following morning leaving Ibarra, Ecuador en route to Bogotá and we didn't realize it until we were halfway back to Guayaquil, might have been an indication that, while the bodies had climbed aboard, the minds had stayed stubbornly behind. Joyce was wrestling with doubts about staying with her boyfriend, and I was checked out of present time in a state of dreamy-eyed infatuation over Heinrich.

Trajectory corrected, and with no other company but our own, we compared notes about the luxury detour with our Swiss hosts. I opened up about what did and didn't happen between Heinrich and me, and she verified reveling in Franz's attention but admitted her heart was still with Alejandro back in Bolivia.

We were now heading north from Ecuador into Colombia, and I can only say in retrospect that bad things can happen when you're checked out of the present, be it from stress, exhaustion—or infatuation!

33

Blindsided in Bogotá

We assessed our finances for the remaining two weeks of travel and came up short, even though we hadn't spent a penny back at Heinrich's gated mansion in Guayaquil. I hadn't needed to pull out my Visa card yet because in those pre-ATM days we still depended on traveler's checks and few businesses accepted credit cards. I tried using my card to pay the hotel bill, but it was rejected. In one of my indignant funks over things not working the way they should, I marched into the nearest local bank displaying a Visa logo only to have the clerk gently point out that my card had expired. *But that can't be because I just got a new one before I left the States!*

As I glared at the date stamped in plastic, the mental tape of what I'd done played back in horrifying slow motion: My replacement card arrived in the mail to my apartment in Sacramento. In anticipation of my upcoming trip to a new continent, I sat at my kitchen table to cut up the old card and put the new one in my wallet. Yes, I scissored up the wrong card.

All these years later, I find it oddly comforting that I could have made such a stupid mistake in my youth. Now it serves as a reminder that maybe today's forgetful errors aren't necessarily a harbinger of the onset of dementia.

The Colombian bank negotiated with Bank of America and agreed to give me cash and charge my B of A account. Whew! That bullet dodged, I walked out with three crisp one-hundred-dollar bills, more than enough to cover the hotel bill, take a short flight to the Caribbean, and buy a nice dinner for Mónica and her husband hosting us in the Dominican Republic, our final destination in Latin America.

Joyce and I were fanatics about finding interesting places to explore wherever we landed, and had read there was a *teleférico* in the hills of Bogotá that offered great views of the city. After changing one of my big bills into Colombian pesos and hiding the other two in our room, we tramped out with map and guidebook in search of the funicular railway to the top for an exciting tram ride back down, not realizing our walking route would take us through a rough neighborhood.

What followed was a four-way collision of unfortunate circumstances. We were in the wrong place, and I was daydreaming of a tall, handsome Swiss man while carrying a small fortune in a bad choice of handbag. Oddly, my mind has always played this scene as viewed from behind, the way the thief would have seen us: strolling through the 'hood, my red wallet secured around my right wrist, my hand forgetting to grip it.

We walk up a narrow street with small houses on both sides. My mind is miles away (though not on the boyfriend back home), but I'm vaguely aware of a woman resting her elbows on the ledge of a Dutch door gazing out at the street as we pass. My reverie is shattered when someone runs up from behind and snatches my wallet dangling from its strap on my wrist, a move perfectly timed as my arm swings back away from my body. Joyce and I whip around but the kid is already running down the hill. In fast pursuit, Joyce grabs his shirt, but he twists away and keeps running. We are only a few strides behind him. I see figures racing toward us and think, "They're coming to our aid!" But no. Our little thief throws an underhand touchdown pass, and I see my red wallet briefly suspended in the air before it lands in the hands of one of his three approaching accomplices.

It is gone, though that doesn't fully register as I lunge airborne at the still-running quarterback. I tackle him around the waist, and we go down hard. With nothing to break my fall, the impact on my shoulder is violent and I can't hold my grip. My body is in shock as he rolls away, jumps to his feet, and runs for his life to catch up with his buddies. Joyce helps me up from the pavement and back onto my feet. We look around for witnesses, but suddenly the street is empty. The Dutch door is closed; there is no one in sight.

We walk until we encounter two policemen and tell them what happened. They accompany us back to the scene of the theft, and to where Joyce had seen the boys disappear into a side street. I show them the Dutch door where the woman had surely witnessed the whole event. They demur when I insist they speak with her. Instead, they drive us to the tourist police office; the judge will be back "*en cinco minutos.*" He returns two hours later after a long lunch and takes our report. We know it is a worthless act, a mere formality in a day's work of recording the complaints of tourists relieved of money, passport, jewelry, and their sense of well-being on the streets of Bogotá.

Joyce and I stopped for coffee to fortify us for the trek back to our hotel. With her characteristic equanimity, she spoke gentle encouragement and reassurances. By then my shoulder ached and I could barely lift the cup. My knee and hip were stiffening from bruises; the hole in my hand stung and was full of dirt. I was a physical, mental, and emotional wreck. Paranoid and scanning everywhere for potential attackers, I burrowed into a dark place in my mind and didn't emerge until two days later when we watched *Midnight Express* at the local cinema. It was a terrifying film about an American college student imprisoned in Turkey after being caught trying to smuggle hashish out of the country. His traumatic experience helped put mine into perspective. I rallied. My physical and emotional pain diminished. We moved on.

After we returned to California, I swore never to return to Colombia. As if to vindicate my vow, the country sank deeper into drug traffic-fueled lawlessness and the terrorism perpetrated by the FARC (Revolutionary Armed Forces of Colombia) and opposing right-wing paramilitaries. The brutal fifty-two-year war of the FARC against the Colombian government officially ended in 2016.

Colombia is now one of the world's premier tourist destinations, with Cartagena hailed as the "queen of the Caribbean coast." However, despite remarkable progress, Colombia remains dangerous due to crime and conflict. It won't be my preferred destination, but I no longer swear I'll never set foot again on Colombian soil because a) we have a dear family friend who insists I must return for *una experiencia magnífica* in his beloved country, and b) what happened on that street could have happened in any number of places on the continent given my fantasy state of mind, unfamiliarity with the neighborhood, carelessness with my wallet, and absence from present time.

It was a frightening and humbling life lesson, and a haunting memory still. Recounting it now in such detail, I feel unsettled on multiple levels. I relive each scene with the stubborn certainty that if I had just done any one thing differently, I could have changed the outcome—a classic in the human bent to argue with what simply *is*. More importantly, If I had reacted differently to the reality of what *was*, I would have accepted it sooner, recovered faster, and could have tuned in to someone else's suffering other than just my own. It wasn't the first time or the last that I was unfeeling toward Joyce, my guilt all the more burdensome for her unwavering sweetness and patience. By some miracle, we remained friends to the end.

34

Caught with the Kilos

We were about to leave the continent for the Caribbean, but Colombia wasn't finished with us yet. Joyce had been generous and patient with me as I pouted and limped my way through a couple of final days in Bogotá. My dark cloud threatened to rain again when our last pass through the post office for general delivery produced no letter from Kevin. That felt ominous, and with more time, distance, and perspective between me and Heinrich, my heart felt heavy for home as we rode in the taxi to the airport.

You will recall that in Lima we had relieved ourselves of thirty pounds in souvenirs and non-essential clothing before our final month of travel—shipped home to California at a high price we were more than willing to pay in exchange for a lighter load. We had acquired little in Ecuador and nothing in Colombia. In fact, I was leaving the country lighter than when I'd arrived, having lost to juvenile thieves my red wallet, its contents of $140 and, I believed at the time, my watch and ring (postscript to follow).

There were duty-free shops in the Bogotá airport, and we opted for a little retail therapy. We found charming kilo packs of Colombian coffee beans in burlap bags with clever little handles, and we each bought two, willing to take on the 4.4 pounds of weight apiece and check off the last names on our family and friends gift lists. We boarded a short flight for our final destination, Santo Domingo, capital city of the Dominican Republic. It was a delight to have checked our luggage and be temporarily separated from those bulky upright suitcases and their useless little wheels.

Of the thirteen nations in the Caribbean Sea, the three largest in area are Cuba, the Dominican Republic, and Haiti, all with populations in the 11 million range. The Dominican Republic shares an island with Haiti, but it is almost twice the size of its western neighbor. Most of my college students correctly answered that Spanish is the language of the DR and French is the language of Haiti. However, this trivia question stumped them every time: What is the actual name of the island the two countries share? Christopher Columbus landed there on December 5, 1492, planted the banner, and claimed it all for the Spanish crown, naming it *La Isla Española* — The Spanish Island, the modern version of which is Hispaniola.

We landed in Santo Domingo in good spirits, knowing that my dear friends, Mónica and Aristides, would meet us at the airport and spoil us for the next few days. Reunited with our luggage, all that remained was to go through customs. Four agents emptied our two suitcases and then had us repack and zip them up before pointing us toward the next station. Maybe this reception was just for travelers coming from Colombia, but Step 2 was another complete review of the contents of our suitcases. Newly zipped, we proceeded to a third station where two more officials opened our small satchels and spread the contents on the table. They looked at each other meaningfully as they pulled each burlap package out of its plastic bag. I explained that we had bought the Colombian coffee as gifts in a duty-free shop at the Bogotá airport. They said that was unfortunate because they couldn't let them pass through. I protested, *"¡Pero son regalos y lo único que contienen es granos de café!"*

They believed me that these were gifts (*regalos*), but they weren't convinced that the only thing they contained was coffee beans. I pleaded as one of them drew a knife from his pocket and sliced open one bag after another. With the table awash in coffee beans, they nonchalantly waved us through. Put to this latest test of things not going the way I was convinced they *should*, I failed another life lesson in equanimity and acceptance in the face of reality. I still had to kick and scream my indignation (on the freedom side of the customs door and mostly in steaming silence) over the unfairness of it all. Yes, we had just arrived from the drug capital of the world, but how could anyone imagine we were anything but innocent tourists? And further, how dare Colombia sell us coffee beans in the airport that wouldn't be allowed through Caribbean customs!

Mónica and Aristides were waiting on the other side of that door, and I just had to believe that we were now fully clear of Colombia with an overwhelming predominance of good times behind us and more yet to come. Yes, the Colombian experience had been traumatic, but after nearly four months of ground travel on an untamed continent, it was the only misfortune that had befallen us. It was time to reflect on all those lucky stars.

Postscript: For security and safety, the first thing I did on arrival in Bogotá was take off my watch and thin gold ring with the tiny diamond set in a circle, seal them into an envelope, and hide that in the lining of my suitcase. We had been warned not to attract attention by wearing jewelry of any kind. Both of these pieces were modest, but they were the costliest things I had ever bought in my young life, and I valued them dearly.

When Joyce and I stumbled back to our hotel after that fateful afternoon on the hill, we found the door to our room wide open. The first thing I did was look for my remaining two one-hundred-dollar bills—Whew! The second thing I did was look for my jewelry, and it was gone from its hiding place. I was at once heartbroken and furious, certain the hotel maid or some passerby had stolen my treasures. The hotel manager was nonchalant when I railed about our door being left open and the absence of my watch and ring.

Two years later, I found a sealed envelope in a small pouch among scraps of paper with addresses, business cards, verses by Pablo Neruda, and international phone prefixes, all gathered on the trek through South America. I never managed to retrace my actions, let alone my thoughts, and can only assume I had moved the envelope out of the suitcase lining and into the scrap pile for better camouflage and, between infatuation with Heinrich and distress over the robbery on cable car hill, had completely forgotten what I had done.

I only stopped berating myself for this years later when friends of mine returned from an extended stay abroad to discover their large fortune of vintage jewelry *gone* from the hiding place they had carefully crafted in their home. Months later, and after police reports and fruitless investigations, they found the entire wealth of gold and precious stones intact in their very own safety deposit box at the bank. In the excitement and stress of leaving the country, they had simply forgotten about their eleventh-hour decision to remove the stash from the house altogether. Embarrassing and humbling—yes, but what a relief to let go of feeling violated *and* have one's treasures back again!

35

The Caribbean Pressure Cooker

The Dominican Republic was suffocatingly hot and humid in August, as it is most months of the year. We had landed in Santo Domingo in the middle of the wet season (May to November) and, although there was little rain during our stay, it was the kind of climate that feels like a perpetual sauna. Mónica said the only difference between the rainy season and the dry season is that the former always delivers more cockroaches and higher humidity. You shower two or three times a day but never feel fresh. You indulge in a perpetual fantasy of lying spread eagle and naked on a huge block of ice. Thankfully, Mónica and Aristides's house had air conditioning and plenty of *small* blocks of ice for lemonade, Perrier, and *Cuba Libre* — rum n' coke.

Since Aristides was now an executive in a multinational company, they lived in relative luxury in what was then a very third-world country but today has become one of the fastest growing economies in the Western Hemisphere. They had a full-time maid, one of whose daily duties was to scrub the shower curtains because mold appeared overnight. There were certainly challenges to living in this small tropical island country, but I could see that the very cosmopolitan Mónica, raised in Chile and schooled in Belgium, was thriving in a new country with her teaching career, her happy marriage (with the first of two daughters soon to be on the way), and their international cluster of friends.

I was enchanted by the story of how they met and have never forgotten the joy of watching my dear friend fall in love. A military coup led by General Pinochet destroyed the democratic government of Chile on September 11, 1973. Anyone suspected of dissent by action or association became a statistic among the many thousands of *chilenos* imprisoned, tortured, or "disappeared" by the regime. The targeted were university students, teachers, artists, activists, and, of course, Communists and Socialists. Having just completed our master's degrees at UC Davis, I moved to Sacramento, Susan back to San Francisco, and Mónica renewed the lease on her apartment. It was clear she would not be going home to a Chile under dictatorship, yet this national tragedy delivered her the gift of staying in Davis to meet her future husband.

She really wasn't in the mood for that party at a friend's place, but she made a reluctant appearance, feeling more frumpy than festive in plain slacks and a black sweater. There, she met the tall, dark, and very handsome graduate student Arístides from the Dominican Republic, and the rest of their history sparked into being. By the time Ari returned to the DR for his new job, they knew they were life partners and Mónica would join him after completing her teaching assignment. The few dollars remaining at the end of the month from her part-time pay were no longer being spent on elegant strappy sandals, but now on functional (but still stylish) sets of kitchen towels and pillowcases.

We saw each other often since we'd both been retained to teach part-time at the University. One day, while visiting at her apartment, she took a phone call from Ari and I overheard her side of the conversation with him in Spanish. It was baffling. Why was she treating him formally, using *usted* for "you" instead of the informal *tú*? After all, it was the twentieth century, and they were engaged. She explained that in Chile, using the formal with one's heartthrob is a form of *coqueteo* (flirting), and is also the way Chilean adults might do baby talk with children and pets. Maybe not the most applicable of linguistic revelations for my developing fluency, but certainly a delightful one. Since my visit in 1979, though we've been together only rarely since then, we've kept in touch by letter and phone. We are the kind of friends who, however long it has been, pick up seamlessly as if we'd never left off.

In Santo Domingo, Joyce and I were reveling in the comforts, the meals, and the delight of afternoon cocktails with Mónica and Ari, but what I really wanted was *her* all to myself—Mónica, that is, not Joyce. Time on the road with one person can stress the fabric of *any* relationship and, after four months, I was feeling pretty threadbare. Surely, Joyce was too.

Perhaps Arístides sensed that my pressure cooker had reached a dangerous level because he volunteered to put through a call to my boyfriend—these things could be easily arranged even in 1979 if you had international business connections. What occurred between Kevin and me in those fifteen minutes felt life-changing. He had been worried over not receiving a letter in weeks and couldn't wait to have me home. I expressed concerns about aspects of my return: Would I get hired back to teach at UC Davis and Sacramento City College? Could I quickly find another restaurant job and an apartment in Sacramento? And where would I stay in the meantime? Legitimate concerns, but really nothing of what was truly weighing on my heart. He said he was weathering storms too but that we had each other after all. I could hardly believe my ears!

Our relationship during the previous four years had been fraught with *altibajos* — the downs of those "ups and downs" fueled by acts which loudly proclaimed lack of commitment. Now, closing the gap between two continents, we taunted and teased each other about would-be romantic liaisons we'd passed up. It was fun and innocent, and I floated down the hall to bed that night feeling light and loved, all worries released for now.

I got up early the next morning, and over breakfast with Mónica, we talked about Kevin and some of the deeply personal experiences I'd had on the road. I still had many things left to say of myself and ask about her, but when Joyce joined us, the conversation turned to neutral subjects. She had her heart set on buying larimar, the rare blue semi-precious stone found only in the Dominican Republic, and off we went on a shopping expedition. In the evening after dinner, Mónica and I retreated to the veranda to smoke cigarettes and talk late into the night. When we were still deep into it at 11:00 p.m., Ari and Joyce gave up on our company and postponed until the next evening a planned excursion to photograph the Colonial City with its buildings dating from the early 1500s, and the New World's oldest paved street from 1502.

After four months living outside of my comfort zone and traveling uncharted paths, I had fewer answers than before. I was filled with a sense of wonder and gratitude that I had actually traversed the whole continent and I felt an abiding optimism for my future, as long as I could keep the nagging questions at bay. I was at once buoyant and mired in doubts—in short, a mass of contradictions. While my conversations with Mónica helped me calm down and gain some perspective, the temperature in my pressure cooker still ran high. Would Kevin and I create a future together? Could I have a viable career as a Spanish teacher without having to endlessly supplement my income with a waitress job? More immediately, could I find a new apartment and start teaching *and* waitressing again right away to pay the rent?

As this adventure of a lifetime was coming to an end, how could I reenter formerly known territory from a different universe and create a new life, while finding ways to freshly relate to what was once familiar? I knew it was useless to try to guess the unknown, and my natural optimism helped me see that some parts of this life puzzle would fall into place naturally, but my future still looked like a Swiss cheese slab of unanswered questions.

36

Taking Flight

Our last evening in Santo Domingo was memorable, not only for delightful company but also because of *merengue* and a flying gecko. We dined with Mónica and Arístides and some of their friends at a trendy outdoor restaurant on the *malecón*, Santo Domingo's oceanfront boardwalk, with the sounds of the sea providing background music to our conversation. When the band started playing after dinner, it was pure *merengue* (meh-REN-ghe), the favored Caribbean rhythm and dance that originated in the Dominican Republic. Couples took to the floor, but none as sensual as Mónica and Ari—their embrace, the rhythmic sway of the hips to match the steps, the shoulders and upper body elegantly motionless. Ocean breezes ruffled Mónica's long, dark hair, and I felt deeply happy that these two marvelous people from separate worlds were building a life together in the DR and that I got to be a part of it, even if just for these few days.

Later that evening, we chatted at home over a nightcap, Joyce and I still refusing to confront the suitcases awaiting our attention. I excused myself to use the bathroom, and as I was walking back through the dim hallway, some *thing* about the size of an open hand fell from above, flopped hard against my chest, bounced off, landed on the floor, and scurried off into the shadows. I ran screaming into the living room and breathlessly stammered out what had just befallen *upon* me. It was no mystery to Mónica and Ari because the geckos come out at night and attach themselves to the walls with

Ari and Mónica in the '80s

their long, sticky, hairy toes and sometimes unexpectedly detach for aerial acrobatics. Geckos heft their heavy tail to right themselves in mid-air and always land on their feet. Harmless though they are, Joyce and I did a thorough search of the bedroom to ensure no reptiles were hitching a ride north in our suitcases. We chatted and laughed while packing, but Joyce grew silent at my mention of her homecoming with Robert.

It's the last leg of our flight home and I am trying to illuminate and examine my hopes and anxieties by writing—always my go-to way of processing. The closer we get to California, the more crystal clear is my resolve:

1. I am fully committed to a career as a Spanish teacher and will keep moonlighting as a waitress as long as it takes to get a full-time college position.
2. I resolve to find out what is causing my constant and worsening skin irritations of nonstop itching. (I suspect a food allergy.)
3. I vow that my next cigarette will be my last.
4. Adventure, defined as *anything* out of my comfort zone, must remain a priority throughout my life.
5. I am in love with Kevin. I read and heard in his words that he has turned an emotional corner, and I am committed to abandoning old hurts and jealousies and beginning anew as true partners.

After a painless pass through customs in the San Francisco airport, I fell into Kevin's arms, just like in the movies. Joyce and Robert were reunited as well and, although they remained friends, their romance did not last much longer. As for the two of us travelers, the airport parting was a confusion of luggage, boyfriends, well-wishes with too much left to say, and the sensation of having a foot in both continents with the land masses slowly moving apart. We said goodbye affectionately, awkwardly, both of us stumbling back into a formerly familiar universe.

Over dinner in an Asian restaurant in nearby Berkeley, Kevin and I explored the events and experiences of four months of absence from the perspective of both sides of the equator and filled in the blanks of the mail that never arrived. After some light banter about how many times either of us could have . . ., I launched the question, feeling queasily compelled, "Have you been with anyone else?" Well, yes he had, with Michele—a past player in his infidelities—quickly adding that it really didn't mean anything because, as he put it, "I didn't even take off my socks." I spent the night on the sofa of our luxurious Berkeley hotel.

We patched things up as I recovered from jet lag, time warp, and a rough reentry into routines and responsibilities. Life sped up again and I found a darling little cottage in mid-town Sacramento, jumped back into multiple part-time teaching assignments for the fall semester with Sacramento City College, UC Davis, and the UC Extension, and started a new restaurant job managing a natural food eatery just a few blocks from my apartment. A few months later, Susan and I started a business of delivering intensive two-week Spanish courses to oil company execs being transferred from Libya in the early 1980s to various Spanish-speaking countries as the U.S. government cut ties with the Libyan leader, Muammar Qaddafi.

Along with hectic normalcy, I still had one psychic foot on another continent. Frequently and unpredictably, I would get a blast of sensory perception from somewhere in South America, a sound, a vision, a taste on my tongue, or a smell that came at me as full and rounded as present physical reality. This was inexplicable, yet so compelling that I would look around my apartment, the restaurant, or my classroom before realizing there was no local source. I came to welcome the phenomena and savor the moments of suddenly being transported to the fish market in Viña del Mar with Mónica's father slurping raw sea urchins, of tasting the savory-sweet Argentine empanada of beef and raisins on a mountainside in Bariloche, of hearing the roar of the crowd chanting samba for "our" team at the *Maracanã* stadium in Río, of smelling the gaucho bonfires that night in Salta. I wanted this to go on forever, but like a dream evanescing in the light of dawn, it diminished over time.

Months after my return, I was having a heart-to-heart talk with a dear friend and mentor over lunch in downtown Sacramento, and the subject of my five-year relationship with Kevin was front and center. He asked me a single question, spawning a personal hurricane that made landfall squarely on my heart: "Where do you see yourself in five years?" I squirmed. I tried to rationalize with the same stupid argument I had started using when the whole affair began, *I'm staying in this until the bad outweighs the good*. I walked out of that café without answering his question, but it haunted me night and day. It burned into my brain and seared my soul.

In the days that followed, I exhausted every defense, rationale, excuse, and delay I could muster. On the day I finally accepted that the answer was crushingly clear, I drove thirty-four miles west on the I-80 to his house. I sat across from him and told him I was leaving. He fell to his knees and begged, I resisted, we hugged, I left. I felt no rancor or regret, just a deep and lonely sadness shadowing the freshly washed window through which I was sure I *couldn't* see myself with him in another five years.

I second-thought it many times when the pain was hard to bear, but I never went back. In the moments of floundering, I made myself look hard at the question, "Will he be here for me?" There was a recent time when I was mugged on the UC Davis campus on an early winter evening while walking to my car after teaching my last class. After an hour in the campus police station and the drive back to Sacramento, I called Kevin in tears at 9:00 p.m. He refused to stay on the phone with me because he had other "pressing matters." His serial faithlessness was blatant in my memory, but most of all I had to accept that I just wasn't cherished. Shortly after my return, I mentioned to him the many five- to ten-page letters I'd written from the road, asking if I might keep the ones that had actually reached him since they were the most detailed journal of my trip. He looked more confused than sorry when he said, "But I read them and threw them away."

37

Reckoning and Redemption

Joyce and I officially finished our four-month South American sojourn in the Dominican Republic on August 10, 1979. August and September were the high hurricane season, but luck was with us once again because deadly "David" didn't hit the Caribbean until later that month. The Dominican Republic was the principal target of massive devastation, and two thousand lives were lost there alone. Flooding swept away entire villages and destroyed 70 percent of the country's crops. The lovely *malecón* where we had strolled along the waterfront every day, and danced merengue on that last evening, was gone in the fury of Category 5 winds and crashing waves. Mónica and Arístides were safe, but the destroyed buildings, damaged infrastructure, and wrecked daily life of this island would take many years to rebuild.

Joyce and I fretted over the large box we had shipped from Lima to her aunt's house in Sacramento, for it hadn't arrived by the end of our first month back home. We didn't care if we never again saw the items of clothing we'd worn to death all over the continent, but the beautiful weavings from Bolivia, the gifts we had received from friends along the way, the lovely artisan crafts we'd bought for friends and family, and Joyce's massive crocheted bedspread were irreplaceable.

When the long-awaited delivery finally arrived shortly before Halloween, we made it into a reunion of sorts. We'd been in touch but hadn't seen much of each other since our return: she, slogging through backlog with her job in California State administration, and I, shuttling from 8:00 a.m. classes at UC Davis to my restaurant job during the day and then out to Sacramento City College locations for the evening session. As we divvied up the goods, we laughed and relived moments from those four months on the road, the tension of too much togetherness having dissipated with distance and daily life.

My biggest purchase during the trip, both in size and expense, was the five-by-seven-foot hand-woven wool tapestry of stylized birds from Bolivia. I was so excited to finally have it in hand, and I tacked it up on the living room wall of my cottage in Sacramento. On an evening soon after its debut, a friend and I were sitting on the sofa and he leaned his head back, looking up at the exquisite piece, and said, "Wow, the air currents in this room are really amazing!" I had no idea what he was talking about and craned my neck to match his gaze behind our heads. Confusion. Disbelief. ¡Qué horror! All over the tapestry were thin, half-inch protrusions waving around in different directions. Worms!

I was paralyzed with revulsion and denial, but Paul was decisive. He stood up to his full six feet and seven inches of height, calmly and oh-so-carefully untacked the weaving from the wall, folded it up with the little intercontinental travelers trapped inside, and helped me seal it into a plastic trash bag. After taking it to the cleaners the next day, I vacuumed and scrubbed every inch of my cottage. The Bolivian birds eventually reclaimed their place of honor in my living room, but not without a major hitch causing a two-month delay. The cleaners had sent my piece to another branch, lost all track and record of its existence let alone its whereabouts, and didn't manage to produce it until I threatened to have them pay for my return trip to South America to purchase a replacement.

Which brings up the subject of me, or what seemed to have become me in the past months. At times on the trip, my personality felt out of control with emotional withdrawals into silence and resentment, or outbursts about things not going the way they "should." I wondered what the hell was wrong and feared I was becoming a bad person. Yet, when not in this depression, I was glorying in the travel experience of a lifetime and grateful for the company of someone as calm and cheerful as Joyce.

Coffee was our most consumed beverage in South America. You might think that was because it was so authentically rich and delicious—far from the truth. I cannot speak to the continent-wide practices in the twenty-first century, but in 1979 all the good coffee was exported and what the locals drank was at best weak and inferior, and at worst, instant. In Chile, Nescafé was on every breakfast table and served in every hotel. In Argentina and Uruguay, two steaming pots were served at breakfast: one of hot milk and the other of watery coffee. Bolivia won our award for the worst coffee and Brazil for the best. In every restaurant in Peru, we were served a cup of hot milk accompanied by a shot glass of cold coffee syrup.

I had been having an annoying skin problem for over a year and realized it had gradually progressed from occasional, to daily, to constant. I often visualized going to bed in a straitjacket because my skin itched so badly, flaring up at any time, but always at night when I undressed, put on my night shirt, and lay in bed. All the "hot spots" were on fire: inside my elbows, behind my knees, the base of my spine, and down the center of my torso. I would lie in bed with my arms behind my back to keep from itching. When I succumbed, there would be red raised bumps and worse irritation.

On our return, I started looking into the effects of food allergies as I had promised myself to do. It was overwhelming, especially in an age before the internet: wheat, soy, corn, pinto beans, strawberries, nuts, shellfish—I had no idea where to start and how to carry out the complicated diet of eliminating and then re-introducing one item at a time. Feeling overwhelmed that autumn with no medical insurance or money for allergy testing, I thought, *The one thing I can do right now is quit drinking coffee.* Within a week, my skin cleared, the hot spots cooled, and my midnight fantasies shifted from straightjackets to more tantalizing images. Caffeine-free, a calmer and kinder me reclaimed the stage while that angry personality melted away like the Wicked Witch of the West.

I know, I know—I promised on the flight back to California from the Dominican Republic that my next cigarette would be my last, and it was—that is, until Kevin revealed his unfaithfulness that "didn't really count" because he didn't remove his socks. Okay, so I used this as an excuse to keep cigarettes in my life and, feeling devastated, reached for the surest and most accessible solace. Before I spent the night on the sofa in our hotel room, I bought a pack in the lobby and consoled myself with a couple of smokes on the balcony. It was another five years before I finally quit that daily habit. And, to add to my embarrassment, I admit that during those five years I was in denial about the incongruity of being a smoker *and* managing a health food restaurant.

38

Valediction for an Odyssey

My mother always said, "You have to balance your head and your hands." Teaching college Spanish and working in restaurants helped me achieve that balance between the intellectual and the physical and ensure a consistent income. However, working the majority of the twenty-four hours seven days a week was a challenge for head, hands, and the rest of me too. The restaurant I was hired to manage in Midtown Sacramento was a homey, natural food eatery with a lot of regular customers and a fairly consistent crew of cooks and wait staff.

I kept my slick Toyota Celica for professional arrivals to college faculty parking lots and acquired a heavy-duty Ford truck for the pick-ups at General Produce. If the opening cook didn't show, I flipped eggs before driving to Davis for my morning class. During lunch rushes, I waited tables and cashiered. After my City College evening classes, I worked in the prep kitchen. If the guy hired to clean the bathrooms at 3:00 a.m. was a no-show, well—you get the idea.

My love for teaching only intensified after the South America trip. When I returned in August, I couldn't wait to meet my new Spanish students now that I had the benefit of improved fluency and an intimate acquaintance with the continent and its many cultures and features that I'd been teaching about with only second-hand knowledge for almost a decade. As a traveler through South America, I'd acquired knowledge, depth, and great stories to share with the thousands of students who were yet to arrive to my classrooms at UC Davis, Sacramento City College, and later, Mendocino College. Whether beginning, intermediate, or advanced level, my enthusiasm for teaching Spanish has never flagged.

As for this recounting of haps and mishaps, of meetings and partings so long ago, I'd always intended to write about them but never did until now. I can't blame that on Kevin who threw away all my letters. My parents saved theirs, and on my first visit home they presented me with an album that had each one of them preserved in plastic pages. Why did I not write these stories then? And why now? Why did I delay forty years to even begin? I could name "reasons," but there are no accidents.

After publishing *Wordstruck! The Fun and Fascination of Language*, I wrote a few travel pieces for my newspaper column, yet I never envisioned penning the entire saga of South America. I published an article about my time in Italy and a few about adventures in Ecuador and Oaxaca with my Mendocino College study/travel students. After I wrote and published two pieces about the 1979 continental odyssey, the lid to Pandora's Box flew open and they just kept coming. Every other weekend I holed up with my laptop, immersed in an alternate universe. I was embodying that past experience so fully that I even started having the sensory flashbacks again, perceiving a smell or a sound that viscerally transported me to 1979 somewhere in the latitudes south of the Caribbean.

Novelists say that characters and plot take on a life of their own and often develop in completely unanticipated directions. I believe them but I haven't a fictional bone in my body or bent in my brain. My South American stories are true to the facts, even though the people I experienced them with, Joyce in the fore, might have very different recollections of events. And, of course, I changed some names to protect people's privacy.

Ultimately, the stories demanded that I write them, unwilling to stay enclosed in memory, journal, or photographs, refusing *not* to be told. All of life's experiences change us. No matter the circumstances, to some degree we are never the same. As Heraclitus said, "No man ever steps in the same river twice, for it's not the same river and he's not the same man." My experiences in South America changed me profoundly and in so deeply cellular and psychic ways that I cannot imagine me without them. You can get off a plane and say, "That was the trip of a lifetime," but you can't call it "life-changing" until you have lived to see life change.

Those four months have informed my life in ways that keep unfolding even decades later: my love of language, my personal relationships, my spiritual life, fascination with cultures, how I see the world, and my attitude about taking risks. What if Joyce and I had let that initial conversation about traveling through South America drift into the dust of "someday"? What if I had been too worried about financial instability to put jobs on hold and fly south to spend all my savings? What if I'd surmised that it was better to stay close to Kevin than to put the boyfriend on the back burner for a season? What if fear of the unknown had won out?

Rarely does one take a wild leap out of their comfort zone and return to say, "I wish I hadn't done that" (though perhaps not so rarely when it comes to risky financial ventures). Life winds down, and it's more likely to hear play the wistful tune, "I wish I had . . .." The German language has a graphic and emotionally charged word for diminishing opportunities with advancing age: *Torschlusspanik*, which translates literally as "gate-closing panic." I'm still an active traveler but have reached an age where I've come to understand well that concept of the slamming gate. In 1979 the gate to South America was flung open, and I am ever grateful and still in awe that I walked through it, and that Joyce did too.

She never went back to Bolivia, but Alejandro visited her in Sacramento a few times. Years after our return, I asked Joyce, "Is there anything you regret?" The answer came in the second part of her reply: "When we returned from South America, I knew I would never marry. I found the love of my life in Bolivia, and he wasn't fully available."

The assigned novel for one of my graduate seminars was by the Peruvian writer Ciro Alegría. It stayed with me not for its plot, but for its title: *El mundo es ancho y ajeno* — The World is Wide and ¿_____? *Ancho* means "wide" but there is no simple English equivalent for *ajeno*, and I kept turning it over in my mind, aiming for a clear concept of meaning and how to properly use it in my second language. It translates as "outside of oneself; belonging to someone else," and suggests alienation and disenfranchisement, which is what the novel portrays in an indigenous community high in the Peruvian Andes. After ten countries and countless unique cultures, I was more in awe than ever of how *ancho* the world really is. As for *ajeno*, I had come to understand the word well enough to know that it was not at all applicable to the sum of my experiences.

For this traveler, teacher, and resident of Earth, those 12,000 land miles manifested a vibrant and vivid reality of peoples, customs, and geography that had been only a vague generality of photographs, words, and maps before I set foot in South America. An entire continent came into being for me, and it was *ajeno* no longer. I owned it. It was and always will be mine.

I turn to the very last page of my travel journal, and trace my finger over the words I wrote so long ago above the map of South America:
"El mundo es ancho y *mío*."

Valediction for an Odyssey

With love and gratitude / In memory of Joyce / 1949-2009

Index

Aguas Calientes, Peru, 97, 99-100, 106
ajeno, 186
ancho, 186
anticuchos, 89
altiplano, 68-69
altitude sickness (see *soroche*)
Antarctica
  territorial claims to, 33, 33n
Argentina, 33-41, 52-67
  dictatorship, 40
Asunción, Paraguay, 48

bank holidays and strikes, 52, 98, 122
Bariloche, Argentina, 34-36
Bogotá, Colombia, 161-168
Bolivia, 68-87
  Bolivian Plateau (see *altiplano*)
  coups d'etat, 76
  minerals, 75
border crossings, 33-34, 138-139
Braniff Airlines, 3
Brazil, 45-47
Buenos Aires, Argentina, 37-41

caballitos de totora, 129-130
caceroladas, 16
capital cities, highest in the world, 139
Caribbean islands, 166
Casa Blanca escape, 83-85
castellano, 45
Cerro Blanco, 124
Chaco War, 49
Chariots of the Gods?, 116-118
Charles Darwin Center, 149
chifas (Chinese diners), 122, 139

Chile, 5-32
  geography, 7, 14
  military coup and dictatorship, 16
    U.S. involvement, 16, 19
Chillán, Chile, 20
Christo's fence, 125
Cien años de soledad, 127
cigarettes (see smoking habit)
Ciro Alegría, 186
chucrut, 23, 34
coca leaves and tea, 62, 75, 98-100, 103
cóctel at the Manchester Café, 43, 88
coffee, 181-182
Colombia, 161-168
  civil war, 164
comfort zone, 2
Corral, Chile, 26
Cotopaxi, 32
cultural *faux pas*, 43-45
Cusco, Peru, 88-99, 114-115

diminutives, 8-9
"disappeared" (*desaparecidos*), 16, 40
Dominican Republic (DR), 166, 169, 179
don and *doña*, 8
Dry Ashlar Construction, 104

Easter Island, 130
Ecuador, 138-160
Ekeko, 80
erizos de mar (see sea uchins)
FARC, 164
Forrest Gump, 13

Galápagos Islands, 14, 141-157
García Márquz, Gabriel, 127
garúa, 128
gauchos, 54-67
geckos, 174-175
Güemes, gaucho hero, 54, 65
grave diggers, 140-141
Guayaquil, Ecuador, 144, 158-160

Haiti, 166
harp (see Paraguayan harp)
Hiram Bingham's Discovery, 104
Hispaniola, 166
honeymooners (see *mieleros*)
Huanchaco, Peru 129
Huayna Picchu, 105-106
Hurricane David, 179

Illimani, 74
Inca empire, 100-101
Inca Trail, 97, 106
Inesita y Juanito, 6-8, 12, 15-17
invitar (to invite), 39

Kosok, Paul, 121

La Calle de las Brujas (The Street of Witches), 78-80
Lake Titicaca, 130
"*La Llorona*," 61
La Paz, Bolivia, 74-85, 87
Lima, Peru, 124-128
loco (shellfish), 12-14, 18
Lonesome George, 152-153, 156-157
luggage, 5, 73-74, 127, 179

Machu Picchu, Peru, 97-107
Man of La Mancha, 127-128
mate (see *yerba mate*)
Méndez Family, Montevideo, 42-43
Mendocino College, 184
mieleros (honeymooners), 35-36
Montevideo, Uruguay, 41-43

Nazca, Peru, 108, 113-125
Nazca Lines/Nazca Plain, 116-123
nicknames, 61-62

ñanduti, 49

Oaxaca, Mexico, 111-112
One Hundred Years of Solitude, 127
Oruru, Bolivia, 69, 71-72
Osorno Volcano, 29-32

Pablo Neruda, 18-19
Pachamama, 80
Paraguay, 48-51
  dictatorship, 49
Paraguayan harp, 49
Patagonia, 7, 20, 25, 29, 33
  Argentine-Chilean dispute, 33-34
  German influence in, 23-25, 34
Peru, 88-109, 114-133
Pinochet, Augusto, 6, 16-17, 19-20, 170
piropos, 131-137
piura, 14
Pizarro, Francisco, 97, 100
Puerto Montt, Chile, 29
pyrotecnics, 90-91

Quito, Ecuador, 139

Reiche, Maria, 121, 123
Rio de Janeiro, 45-47

Saquisilií, Ecuador, 140-141
Sacramento City College, 3-4, 177, 180, 184
Salta, Argentina, 52-67
Salvador Allende, 16, 18-19
sandboarding (see sand dunes)
sand dunes, 124
Santiago, Chile, 5-6
Santiago Rojas, 20-21
Santo Domingo, DR, 15, 165-166, 171-175
sauerkraut (see *chucrut*)

sea urchins (*erizos de mar*), 14
sense of direction, 85-87, 109-113
Shining Path (*Sendero Luminoso*), 126
smoking habit, 28, 176, 182
sobremesa, 10
sobrenombres (see nicknames)
soccer (*futebol*), 46-47
soroche (altitude sickness), 75, 82
soup pot, 91-96
South American Handbook, 5, 34, 70, 139
Southern Cross, 70
"Stairs of Death," 105-106
Stroessner, Alfredo, 49
suitcases (see luggage)

tango, 40, 42-43
Temuco, Chile, 21, 23
tortoises, 152-157
totora reed, 129-130
Trujillo, Peru, 129
tú (see *usted* vs. *tú*)

UC Davis, 4, 20-21, 170-171, 177, 180
Uruguay, 41-43
usted vs. *tú*, 7, 170

vaccines, 41
Valdivia, Chile, 22
Videla, Jorge Rafael, 40
Villazón, Bolivia, 69, 81
Villarica, Chile, 22, 23, 29
Viña del Mar, Chile, 6, 15
volcanoes, 68-69
Von Däniken, Erich 116-118

War of the Pacific, 75-76
War of the Triple Alliance, 48-49
wheel, invention of, 73
witches (see *La Calle de las Brujas*)
Wonders of the World, 104

yerba mate, 54, 62-64

zampoña (panpipes), 71

Acknowledgments

Once the manuscript is completed, that's when the author needs a village. I am delighted to report that mine has been stellar with enthusiasm, talent, inspiration, and generosity.

Before there was a book, I wrote a few articles about travels through South America in my column in our local newspaper. With feedback and encouragement from readers, I began to see a bigger picture and took on the challenge of writing a complete account of the entire odyssey. I thank all of you who read and resonated with those early travel tales in my column, for they were the seeds of the book now before your eyes.

I am grateful for the work of David Aretha, my editor, and to fellow author, Karen Rifkin, for recommending him to me. As I polished chapter after chapter, my dear friend Wendy DeWitt, the renowned "Queen of Boogie Woogie," found time between gigs to read them and offer valuable insights and corrections. Later in the process, Dr. Glenn Rogers, author of a terrific Spanish-English medical dictionary, resolved my dilemma of how to quote words, phrases, and dialogue in two languages. I am indebted to Jody Gehrman, award-winning playwright and novelist, for years of inspiration as my office neighbor at Mendocino College, and because she exhorted me to tell the whole story, dirty socks and all.

I am truly indebted to my publishing consultant, Martha Bullen of Bullen Publishing Services, whose talents would fill a chapter. *Once Upon a Continent* would never have materialized from the mists of time had it not been for her energy, perception, vast store of experience and knowledge, clarity, attention to detail, and her kind but firm direction to keep me on the timeline.

Christy Day of Constellation Book Services is the magician I thank for the book cover and interior design. Christy and her associate Bertha Edington seamlessly handled the many details of publishing both a print and an ebook. Along with Martha Bullen, they formed my publishing dream team.

If you enjoy the many photos throughout my chapters, that is thanks to David Nelson for his amazing image mastering of a pile of ancient slides and snapshots. The higher resolution and fresh clarity he achieved make the photos sing beyond my wildest dream in both the print book and ebook.

In addition to the love and support of all the Janssens, I especially want to thank my brother Fred for cheerleading from his heart, problem-solving my tech issues from his head, and being my cherished friend from his soul. Sarah Katherine Janssen, my niece and Fred's daughter, is an artist of the highest order. Her hand-drawn map makes my trajectory around the continent trackable and helps my story come alive for readers. Also for Sarah: deep gratitude for artistic feedback on possible cover images, and for talking me through the essence of my experience in South America to the deeply symbolic image of the volcano that embodies what this trip meant for me. In addition to her many talents, nobody races up and down sand dunes in the Sahara like Sarah.

I am grateful for the warmth and support of my graduate school friends and professors, all of whom played vital roles in my bilingual path and teaching career. Special thanks to the major players who made this a memoir and not just a travelogue: Susan, Mónica and her husband, Arístides, and, of course, Kevin! Most of all to sweet, intrepid, and strong-as-steel Joyce to whom this memoir is dedicated. She did not survive to see it published, but she lives forever in these pages and in my heart.

Final thanks with hurrahs to you, my readers, for signing on to this once-upon-a-time odyssey around a continent. You are the reason it is in print and not just in my memory.

About the Author

SUSANNA JANSSEN is a wordsmith, world explorer, and lifelong language enthusiast who believes that words and the comfort zone exit door are the passports to adventure. Early in her teaching career, she traveled throughout South America for four months—an experience that transformed her into a master teacher and has shaped her life ever since. That odyssey is fully revealed for the first time in *Once Upon a Continent: A Memoir of South American Adventures Unplugged.*

A retired college professor turned dynamic language coach, she teaches Spanish and Italian, helping learners unlock fluency with flair. As the founder of Novelas en Español, she creates immersive resource packages that turn reading authentic Spanish novels into accessible, engaging journeys for language learners.

A passionate advocate for reading as an ever-thrilling love affair, Susanna feeds the brain, warms the heart, and tickles the funny bone with her first book, *Wordstruck! The Fun and Fascination of Language*, winner of five national awards in Humor and Education.

She honed her skills and delighted readers as a newspaper columnist, weaving stories of words, language quirks, cultural curiosities, and travel escapades.

When she's not writing, teaching, or coaching, you'll find Susanna planning her next exploration or being whisked away by curiosity to destinations unknown. Whether entertaining an audience with the magic of language or elaborating on the fine points of Spanish grammar, she brings an infectious enthusiasm that makes every encounter a linguistic adventure.

From her home in Northern California, Susanna continues to ignite a passion for words and cultures, knowing that learning never stops, and that adventure can be reading a good book in a comfy armchair or sailing a frigate on the high seas. It exists wherever you create it.

To learn more or contact Susanna, visit susannajanssen.com.

www.ingramcontent.com/pod-product-compliance
Lightning Source LLC
Chambersburg PA
CBHW051605010526
44119CB00056B/789